All together

How to create inclusive services for disabled children and their families

2nd edition

Mary Dickins with Judy Der

national
children's
bureau
making a difference

The National Children's Bureau promotes the interests and well-being of all children and young people across every aspect of their lives. NCB advocates the participation of children and young people in all matters affecting them. NCB challenges disadvantage in childhood.

NCB achieves its mission by
- ensuring the views of children and young people are listened to and taken into account at all times
- playing an active role in policy development and advocacy
- undertaking high quality research and work from an evidence based perspective
- promoting multidisciplinary, cross-agency partnerships
- identifying, developing and promoting good practice
- disseminating information to professionals, policy makers, parents and children and young people.

NCB has adopted and works within the UN Convention on the Rights of the Child.

Published by the National Children's Bureau, Registered Charity number 258825. 8 Wakley Street, London EC1V 7QE. Tel: 020 7843 6000. Website: www.ncb.org.uk

© National Children's Bureau 2003
All revisions to the 1998 edition (published by the National Early Years Network) have been made by Mary Dickins.

Published 2003

ISBN 1 900990 92 X

British Library Cataloguing in Publication Data
A catalogue record for this book is available from the British Library

Cover photograph by Jacky Chapman.

Contents

Dedication

This book is dedicated to Jeanne Smythe who died in July 2001. Jeanne was a valued friend and colleague who spent most of her professional life striving to improve the quality of life for disabled children and their families. During that time she influenced many people, especially in terms of her commitment and sheer humanity. Jeanne was a very modest person and a relatively unsung heroine. She will be sorely missed but never forgotten by all those who knew her.

Thanks also to Ann Robinson for her invaluable help in updating and researching useful organisations and sources of training and support.

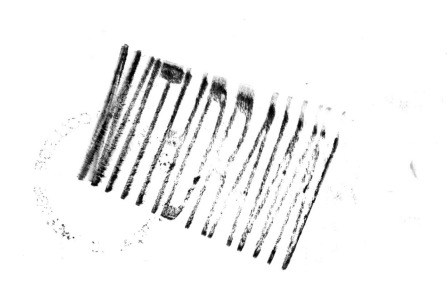

Notes on this publication

Terms used

- 'Disabled child' is our preferred term of reference, not because we wish to define children in terms of what society sees as their shortcomings, but because this is the terminology that disabled people have chosen. They are proud to be themselves. This is the language of the disability movement and we respect it.
- 'Special educational needs' (SEN) is used only because it is the wording of the legislation. 'Special needs' is not used. For a longer explanation, see the section 'Special needs' on page 9.
- Where possible and appropriate we use the term 'entitlement(s)' rather than 'need(s)'. The idea that some children might have 'needs' implies a deficiency on the part of those individual children, whereas all children have an equal 'entitlement' to quality services. The term 'entitlement' therefore ensures that disabled children and those with other forms of SEN are not set apart from the population of children as a whole.

References

References to publications are shown in brackets as the author followed by the date of publication, for example (Smith 1996). The relevant book or article can be found in the 'References and further reading' section on page 133.

Introduction

If a man does not keep pace with his companions,
perhaps it is because he hears a different drummer.
Let him step to the music which he hears, however
measured or far away.
Henry David Thoreau (1840)

This publication has four aims:

- to remind readers that disabled children are children first, sharing the same needs and desires as all children
- to promote the ideals and principles of inclusion in the care and education of young disabled children
- to provide information about current legislative requirements and their implications
- to give practical advice on how to create an inclusive early years setting.

We wish to encourage those who work with children to examine their attitudes and assumptions, to extend their skills and develop new ones. We wish to enable managers and staff to develop policies that are well-thought-out and comprehensive. Most of all, we wish to promote the view that each disabled child is a unique individual rather than part of a homogeneous group that it is possible to make generalisations about.

We see inclusion as a human right, with benefits for all concerned.

In the past, society put disabled children and adults away in institutions. Today, although there have been many improvements, we still sometimes segregate children at an early age even though most academics, practitioners and politicians agree that this is not what is best for them.

We are in a time that offers challenges as well as opportunities. Inclusion is now part of central government policy. Discrimination against disabled children and their families is, from 2003, unlawful and open to legal challenges as disability rights legislation has been widened to include educational establishments within its remit. We hope early years practitioners will join in the process of change that can help to develop a much healthier society.

Disability is a field in which a little knowledge can be a dangerous thing. Early years practitioners often think that in order to include disabled children they must immediately increase their knowledge of various syndromes, specialised equipment and medical procedures. There is undoubtedly a bewildering multitude of conditions, but while some knowledge of a particular syndrome and condition may be necessary for individual physical care, too great a focus on medical details can lead to over-generalisation and place limitations that do not necessarily apply to a particular individual. A better approach is:

- to acquire such knowledge at the point when you need it to support an individual child rather than trying to do so as part of general training
- to build your skills and knowledge through direct experience with an individual child, because all children constantly challenge assumptions that adults make about them
- to make the child's parents your primary source of information

- to make professional links and build positive relationships with those who are part of the wider team that are caring for a child.

This publication does not tell you about specific medical conditions or syndromes, nor about complex procedures or equipment, although it tells you where to get that information if you really need it. Instead, we hope it will help you to see beyond the disability and find ways of reaching each individual child with greater confidence.

We hope that, in the future, every child will be able to take a full part in all the social and learning experiences that will help them maximise their potential for achievement in later life.

Mary Dickins and Judy Denziloe, 2003

1 What is disability?

Disability is a range of difficulties on a continuum that spans minor impairments, such as mild long-sightedness in middle age, through to profound and multiple disabilities that have a major impact on quality of life.

Viewed in this way it becomes clear that disability is a feature of ordinary life that will touch all of us at some point, directly or indirectly. This is a very different perception from the one that fears disability as unfamiliar, confuses it with illness, chronic disease and mental disorders, and creates the prejudice that surrounds and sometimes engulfs disabled people.

How we understand disability

Throughout history, society has sought to explain disability to itself. These explanations have narrowed into three main alternatives, or models, for how people might view disability in the UK today.

The religious model

Disability is a punishment for 'evil' behaviour. Disabled people and their families are stigmatised and avoided. Although this may seem an archaic notion, vestiges of the idea still exist in many societies and cultures, including our own – though they may not be overtly expressed. The fact that they have grown out of the religious concepts of 'good' and 'evil' does not mean that these beliefs are held only by religious people. They are more general than that, and sometimes manifest themselves in parental guilt and soul-searching at having given birth to a child with a disabling condition.

In this model the child is seen as a punishment.

The medical model

The medical model of disability has informed much of our thinking, policy-making and professional practice over the past century. The assumption is that, because disability is caused by mental or physical impairments, then it is a medical 'problem' that we must 'treat'. Doctors must attempt to cure or alleviate the effects of such impairments and it is their job to make the child more 'normal'.

While there is nothing at all wrong with alleviating suffering or discomfort, the main problem with this model is that the impairments are the sole focus of attention. The child becomes a set of problems rather than an individual with strengths and weaknesses to be welcomed into the world with joy and anticipation. This model leads us down the road of 'quick fix' thinking that early interventions can take care of all the 'problems' (see 'Early intervention and inclusion' on page 7).

In this model the child is seen as faulty.

The social model

In the social model the 'problem' is located outside the province of disabled people and their families, and back into the collective responsibility of society as a whole. In this model, it is the social and physical barriers that society creates which are disabling. Micheline Mason (1993), a leading campaigner for the rights of disabled people, puts it like this:

> Disabled people's own view of the situation is that whilst we may have medical conditions which hamper us and which may or may not need medical treatment, human knowledge, technology and collective resources are already such that our physical or mental impairments need not prevent us from being able to live perfectly good lives. It is society's unwillingness to employ these means to altering itself … which causes our disabilities.

The social model of disability enables us to accept and value difference. Its goals are already being achieved in pockets of good practice in the UK and all over the world.

In this model the child is valued.

Early intervention and inclusion

A preoccupation with early identification and early intervention for disabled children runs as a strong current through recent early years guidance such as the Early Years Development and Childcare Partnerships planning guidance, initiatives like Sure Start programmes, and even the SEN Code of Practice and associated legislation.

The term 'early intervention' needs urgent unpicking, because our current use of the term serves as an umbrella for anything from parental support and behavioural methods of dealing with challenging behaviour, to radical 'therapeutic' methods such as Dolman Delcato (an intensive therapy treatment requiring input from so many people that it usually involves strangers).

There are excellent and effective interventions, such as Portage (see page 116) and High/Scope (see Appendix 1, page 114), which could be expanded – but other interventions may range from benevolent to positively malevolent and intrusive.

We need to ensure that any intervention we undertake for children in our settings is truly enabling and not destructive to the development of a positive identity and self-image. We need to question a focus that has as its primary roots in the medical model, and temper our zeal for a 'quick fix' solution to children's 'problems' by listening more carefully to the voices of disabled adults and older children who have experienced some interventions as divisive, discouraging and downright humiliating.

The power of words

I am not a disability, I'm me. I have dyslexia and I've had polio but I'm not 'a dyslexic' or 'a cripple', I'm me.
John Swan, aged 14 (Reiser and Mason 1992)

'Politically correct' terminology is constantly being modified; it is governed by social and political forces and is therefore subject to change. This is not a reason to give up on it. It is a mark of respect to the individual or group of people concerned to describe them as they would describe themselves and not to use terminology that they may find objectionable. As well as the words that we use, we must also be aware of the subtle messages we may give through eye contact (or lack of it), body language and tone of voice.

Terminology to avoid

The following terms are labels and have negative associations:

- mental handicap
- the disabled
- the handicapped
- wheelchair-bound
- wheelchair child
- spastic
- suffers from cerebral palsy/spina bifida
- epileptic
- diabetic
- dumb.

Terminology to use

These terms are non-labelling and have more positive connotations:

- disabled people
- people with disabilities
- uses a wheelchair
- is a wheelchair user
- person with cerebral palsy/spina bifida
- person who has epilepsy/diabetes
- uses sign language
- has a speech impediment.

'Special needs'

All children are individual and special, and so are their needs. But the term 'special needs' marginalises disabled children and suggests that their needs are different from everyone else's. It also has very general applications, not necessarily related to disability, which can include children with emotional and behavioural difficulties, those with mental health problems, those whose first language is not English, travellers and so on. This term can be interpreted in so many different ways that it ceases to be helpful. The term 'additional needs' is increasingly being used instead of 'special needs' as an attempt to address some of the problems.

In the language of education legislation the term 'special educational needs' is widely used and it is here that the word 'special' acquires a more negative association. In this context, the term 'special' suggests 'different' and 'separate' rather than 'out of the ordinary' in a positive sense. The term has been used from time to time in this publication because it is the language used in the legislation and is therefore difficult to avoid.

Disabled children and choice

We often take for granted the ability to make effective choices and engage in sensible decision-making processes. But this ability demands skills and experiences that others have enabled us to acquire. These opportunities are crucial for all children, but there are particular issues for young disabled children and the adults they will eventually become. For example:

- disabled children are subject to a much higher degree of adult intervention, so their opportunities for making day-to-day choices are often severely limited
- disabled children are statistically more vulnerable to abuse than non-disabled children
- they are more likely to receive a number of medical interventions and treatments
- they are more likely to be subject to various kinds of assessment procedure
- where there are specific communication difficulties, disabled children are less likely to be consulted
- parents and practitioners are often quicker to step in as advocates for disabled children.

Narrow attitudes towards disability, such as those created through the religious and medical models, have encouraged us to be prescriptive in our attitudes towards disabled people, and to limit opportunities for their preferences and opinions to be expressed and acted upon.

It is important that we do not let perceived communication barriers and difficulties prevent us from enabling children to develop skills that could be crucial to their future fulfilment and independence. After all, research suggests that, regardless of culture and spoken language, communication of any message is approximately 7 per cent verbal (words only), 38 per cent vocal (including tone of voice, inflection and other sounds), and 55 per cent non-verbal (body language, gestures and non verbal cues) (Mehrabian 1971).

The following simple rules can help us communicate with children for whom speech and language may be a barrier:

- get as much information as you can from parents, professionals and other carers about how the child communicates
- establish the child's means of communicating 'yes' and 'no' – this might be blinking or even sneezing
- incorporate a range of familiar objects of reference (toys, photographs, etc.)
- above all, ensure that you consider the level and range of choice afforded in any planned activity and maximise opportunities for all of the children involved.

Self-esteem

There is a consensus between educators at all levels that positive self-esteem is a crucial factor in successful learning for the young child. From birth, children are in the process of belonging and connecting to the world, and of being and becoming themselves as unique individuals, with unique potential and unique destinies.

There is also a consensus regarding those factors which provide an emotional and physical environment that is most helpful for developing a positive identity and the higher levels of self-esteem which accompany it. These factors are:

- close early attachment to parents, family members and carers
- positive and loving relationships with parents, family members and carers
- consistent caring and setting of boundaries
- a safe base from which to explore
- effective communication
- positive relationships with peers, including close friendships
- a positive environment where achievements are valued
- an ability to deal with feelings (emotional literacy).

If each of these factors is examined in the light of the common experiences of disabled children, and particularly if they are in a segregated environment, it becomes clear just how many extra hurdles these children face in developing a positive sense of identity. For example, the bonding process is much more likely to have been interrupted for disabled children, they are more likely to be over-protected, to have communication difficulties, to have a fragmented and restricted educational experience and to be isolated, with fewer friendships. Their educational and developmental achievements are less likely to be valued or praised and more likely to be defined by what they *cannot* do.

There is much that early years settings can do to counter this trend and help children negotiate the hurdles. All children benefit from an environment that:

- welcomes children and their families
- treats children respectfully as individuals
- creates an environment where each child belongs
- provides consistent boundaries
- is supportive, enabling and encouraging
- values achievements
- allows children to make choices
- allows children to take risks
- allows children to learn from mistakes
- creates an environment where children can learn from each other
- values the contribution that families can make
- provides families with information and support.

Disabled children and play

When asked about their memories and early experiences of play, most adults talk about pretend games, being in a gang, building dens, playing with mud, playing with water, and so on. Of course, their response depends to a certain extent on when they were a child, where they lived and the number of other children around, but the list is almost always the same. For most people, the experiences they remember most vividly were not directed by adults and did not include brand-name toys. The memories that we value are about activity, risks, challenges, imagination, creativity and excitement. They are about learning from what happens and finding out how to get on with people.

But what is play like for disabled children?

Whereas play should involve challenge, excitement and risk, disabled children are often protected from physical risk, the risk of failure and the possible unkindness of society. When people recall their most valued play experiences, it usually involves being with friends. Disabled children often find themselves restricted to organised group situations such as school or holiday play schemes. They may be segregated into groups with other disabled children, and it may be difficult to keep friendships going outside the group sessions because of problems such as transport. Opportunities for development can be lost if, for example, children with delayed language are put together. Their primary need to hear language used well in a variety of situations will not be met.

Most disabled children have a lot of adult intervention in their lives, even while they are playing. While adult support may be necessary and unavoidable we must also respect the need for privacy and be ready to withdraw when possible.

A lot of marketing is devoted to the idea that special toys and equipment are needed for disabled children to play with. These items are often more expensive than mainstream toys and we must question their value and their necessity. Very few of us have fond memories of putting plastic pegs in a pegboard or completing an inset board puzzle – yet for many disabled children this type of skill-learning may form a large part of their play experience. Such activities have value, but there must be a balance. This is not to say that all disabled children can, or should, climb trees simply because this is a valued play memory for their carers. But it is possible to examine what is involved in the activity of climbing trees and then to incorporate these experiences into a disabled child's play. A new activity might therefore attempt to involve:

- physical effort
- risk
- excitement
- testing yourself
- being hidden from the world
- looking down at people

- the rustle of leaves and texture of bark
- wind on your face.

Barriers to the play experience

Some disabled children don't seem to know how to play. This could be due to any, or all, of a number of factors.

- Lack of experience and opportunity can lead to lack of motivation.
- For some children, play may be painful and tiring.
- Children may have experienced failure and feel that if they don't attempt something then at least they can't fail.
- Declining abilities, due to a progressive condition, can cause children to feel frustrated when they play.
- Children with a sensory impairment, a learning disability or autism may perceive the world as a chaotic and confusing place. This might cause them to withdraw or exhibit behaviour that is stereotypical to their disability or syndrome as a means of understanding, controlling or shutting out the world.
- The intrinsic rewards of play may be limited so the child may need more external rewards such as toys which move, flash with lights, vibrate or make sounds.

Adults who work with disabled children need to develop skills to support play without taking over. We must create an atmosphere of fun and enjoyment so that children who have been stunted in their natural spontaneity are given the opportunity to begin to play again.

The right to cultural differences

Without effective communication there is always a risk that parents and professionals will have different perceptions of an individual child's needs and of other issues that concern her. But the scope for misunderstanding is even greater when the family and the professional are from different cultural or ethnic backgrounds.

It is all too easy for us to make assumptions about a family's attitude or approach to disability, based on stereotypical views of any particular minority ethnic group. Perhaps you may have heard the following:

'Disability is considered shameful in their culture.'

'In their culture fathers take no interest.'

'Black families don't want support because they look after each other.'

Such popular myths and generalisations are entirely unhelpful when applied to the unique reality of an individual family. Culture has immense impact on child development and behaviour management. But while it is important to respect and value diversity, it is vital to see the individual family rather than just its language or colour – in exactly the same way as we must strive to see the individual child rather than the disability.

In her book *Honouring diversity*, Madeleine Greey (1994) makes the following observations:

Cultural sensitivity means recognising that cultural differences as well as similarities, exist. It means refusing to attach labels, such as better or worse, more or less intelligent, or right or wrong, to cultural differences. They are simply differences. Cultural sensitivity requires that the infant worker not only recognises cultural differences, but also respects the strengths and legitimacy of different cultural practices. People are entitled to be different.

Cultural sensitivity means becoming a better observer of a family's day to day routines. It means learning as much as possible about different cultures and recognising the way culture influences personal thinking, behaviour and values, but recognising that it shows 'tendencies' rather than 'absolutes'. When an infant worker is culturally sensitive, she is aware of cultural possibilities and can respond appropriately with many different strategies. She has an open, non-judgmental mind with no cultural expectations.

Cultural sensitivity is a process approach, rather than a recipe for work with families and children with disabilities and other forms of SEN. There are no simple answers that work universally.

Early years practitioners who are trying to establish and develop good practice may find the following guidelines useful.

- Recognise that black and minority ethnic disabled children and their families face discrimination because of the personal and institutional prejudice and racism that exists in our society. (See Lane (1999) for an explanation of institutional discrimination.)
- Remember that within any community there are always a variety of outlooks, value systems, degrees of awareness and so on.
- Recognise that people from minority ethnic groups are facing a double disadvantage: not only do they have to cope with a lack of understanding regarding their disability, they also face a lack of understanding and sometimes even

animosity towards their culture and language.
- Avoid making assumptions and approach each family and each child as individuals. In this way we can apply whatever knowledge or experience we may have regarding a particular community, but only when it is appropriate.

2 What is inclusion?

*We dream for our children and for your children, for our
children's children and for your children's children. We
dream that children who are labelled, like our children
are today, will one day be included without the slightest
surprise, debate or controversy.*
SNAG Parents Group (Murray and Penman 1996)

Inclusion is about building a community that accepts and values
differences. It is about every part of life, not just education –
although an inclusive education is vital if children are to achieve
a common understanding. A growing number of people believe
that inclusion has the potential to become our most powerful
tool in changing society's attitudes towards disability and
combating the injustices and inequalities that result.

When thinking about what inclusion means, it is useful to
clarify the difference between 'integration' and 'inclusion',
especially as the terms have often been used interchangeably
in the past. Crudely put, 'integration' means placing the child
in a mainstream setting and expecting him to adapt or 'fit in'
as best he can. 'Inclusion', however, means placing the child
in a mainstream setting and instigating a process of change at
institutional and individual level that will enable him to
participate as fully as possible. Change must involve all the
stakeholders in the provision.

Integration puts the onus on the child to adapt and change.
It fails to encourage or facilitate the kind of wholesale change
in attitudes that must underpin successful inclusion. In an

Thoughts on inclusion

The lobbying and support group Parents for Inclusion offer us these thoughts, gathered in a workshop, on what inclusion means for them and their children.

Inclusion is:
- more than integration
- young people taught together in ordinary classrooms
- specialist support brought to the child
- changing ordinary schools
- focusing on a child's strengths and abilities
- all young people learning about the history of disabled people
- accepting difference as ordinary, and not an excuse to dismiss, reject or ridicule
- young disabled people never being forced to live separate lives away from their families and communities
- young disabled people getting the full and effective education they need to lead full and effective lives as adults
- valuing and acting upon the views of young disabled people and children.

Inclusion is not:
- placing children in special units on the site of mainstream provision
- placing children in mainstream provision without appropriate support
- placing children in mainstream provision without due attention to their individual support needs
- placing children in mainstream provision for only part of the day or week (although this may be perfectly appropriate as a short- or even longer-term settling measure)
- placing one or two children in mainstream provision without appropriate SEN and inclusion policies, and no equal opportunities approach.

inclusive model, attitudes, policies and practices may need to change in order to ensure success. This may seem a burdensome process, but its saving grace is that everybody involved stands to benefit (see 'Inclusive early education', page 24).

The campaigning group Alliance for Inclusive Education has adopted the following useful definition of inclusion, and associated principles.

> Inclusive education enables all students to fully participate in any mainstream early years provision, school, college or university. Inclusive education has training and resources aimed at fostering every student's equality and participation in all aspects of life in the learning community.

Inclusive education aims to equip all people with the skills needed to build inclusive communities. It is based on eight principles:

1 A person's worth is independent of their abilities and achievements.
2 Every human being is able to feel and think.
3 Every human being has a right to communicate and be heard.
4 All human beings need each other.
5 Real education can only happen in the context of real relationships.
6 All people need support and friendship from people their own age.
7 Progress for all learners is achieved by building on things people can do rather than what they can't.
8 Diversity brings strength to all living systems.

To achieve this, disabled children must have access to quality mainstream education.

The drive towards inclusive education

When the first edition of this book was written, in 1997, inclusion was considered a radical and almost subversive concept. Since the 1999 Department for Education and Employment SEN Programme of Action it has become official government policy. This welcome drive towards inclusive education on the part of government has brought with it complications and inconsistencies.

- There is still no statutory definition for inclusion, and there continues to be a lack of consensus about its meaning and direction. One example of this confusion is manifested in our treatment of children with emotional and behavioural difficulties (EBD), who are often excluded.
- Local education authorities are working towards inclusion at different speeds and using a range of approaches, sometimes without a clear and coherent strategy. This may result in a lack of vision about transferring the expertise currently held in special schools and provisions into mainstream provision.
- Real inclusive education values achievements which are meaningful for individual children. This can be difficult to equate with a goal-oriented education system which values achievements that have been set as measurable objectives

A working definition of Inclusion

In June 2003 the Early Childhood Forum at NCB held a seminar on inclusion, where the following working definition of inclusion was agreed:

> ECF believes inclusion is a process of indentifying, understanding and breaking down the barriers to participation and belonging.

for all children. Practitioners face a potential contradiction when their settings are encouraged to be inclusive but also high-achieving.

- We still lack the common language and principles needed to carry the work forwards. The language and concepts used in SEN policy and practice are sometimes unhelpful in terms of meeting children's entitlements and helping educational settings towards inclusion. For instance, there is still no cross-sector agreement on what constitutes a 'disability'. The problem is compounded when different agencies concerned with disability and SEN use different terminology and definitions.
- There is a danger that a new tier of segregation could emerge which would encompass severely disabled children and others whose needs are complex and challenging.

Legislation over the past 20 years has emphasised the notional right of all parents to have a choice of provision for their child. During the same period, the academic, philosophical, ideological and political battles to support inclusion have largely been won.

Despite all this, many families still struggle to have their children included in mainstream education, and to get effective support in place. We are still engaged in a debate around the contentious practical issues of how mainstream provision can effectively deliver the specialist services which are necessary, especially in terms of the following.

1 **Cost implications** – We need to remember how costly segregation has actually been. Using transport as an example, we could save an enormous amount of money if we no longer placed children in designated provisions far from their homes and communities.

2 **The need for a shift in resources from special education to mainstream provision** – An enormous amount of expertise and experience has traditionally been held by professionals who operate within the context of special educational provision. The transfer of skills and knowledge into the mainstream sector has already begun and needs to be accelerated in many areas in order to support successful inclusive education.

3 **Fears that including disabled children will somehow dilute the educational achievements of schools** – The London Borough of Newham has had an inclusive education policy since 1985. The most recent statistics to emerge indicate that there has been a rise in the educational achievement levels of all children in Newham.

As a society, we have a duty to listen to the body of disabled people who were educated in a segregated environment and are now clamouring for effective inclusive policies and practices to be introduced. They have a tremendous amount to contribute to our knowledge and understanding of what it is to grow up and be educated as a disabled child. We must listen to the parents who demand choice as their right. We must also take into account the small but significant minority of children whose complex needs will present us with some unfamiliar and difficult challenges as we work towards an inclusive system.

Inclusive early education

It is now universally accepted as good practice for disabled pre-school children to attend mainstream provision wherever possible, and much of the legislative infrastructure needed to support this development is in place. Our challenge now is to do it well.

Nurseries and playgroups are generally smaller, more manageable institutions than schools, so it is often easier for them to achieve the basic conditions for successful inclusive practice.

Real inclusion in the early years offers potential benefits for everyone:

- disabled children benefit from contact with their non-disabled peers in terms of communication skills and social and emotional development
- non-disabled children and practitioners benefit from the change in attitude that familiarity and acceptance can bring – they learn to look beyond disability, focusing instead on a unique and valued person, thereby enriching their own lives
- parents of disabled children are able to become more active members of their local community, thereby suffering less from the isolation that segregated services can bring
- families with a disabled child who have had a positive pre-school experience are more likely to opt for mainstream provision at the primary school stage
- good practice in the care and education of disabled children often improves practice for all children; innovations and adaptations aimed at supporting the inclusion of disabled children often make learning more accessible and enjoyable for everybody.

3 Laws and guidance that support disabled children and promote inclusion

Legislation can seem remote from the real experiences of children and their families, but it is vital for underpinning any useful change within society.

Current legislation should be seen in a historical context as part of a slow process of change for the better. Until 1970, many disabled children were considered ineducable. For many years they were either segregated in special hospitals and institutions or left in the community with little in the way of support or services. Many survivors of these segregated regimes are now adults who can testify to the isolating and damaging effects of such practices.

International initiatives

The following initiatives have no legal force, but they have had some impact on government policy and guidance, including the 2002 revision of the Code of Practice for Children with Special Educational Needs (see pages 38–43).

United Nations Convention on the Rights of the Child

This is by far the most widely agreed international treaty, having been ratified by every UN member state except for Somalia, which has no government, and the United States of America, which does not ratify UN treaties.

The Convention is a human rights treaty used by countries around the world to help promote the rights of children, strengthen government efforts to serve families and build upon the efforts of non-governmental organisations on behalf of children. It sets forth basic norms and standards in a number of articles, which individual nations agree to pursue on behalf of their children. These norms include:

- protection from violence, abuse and abduction
- protection from hazardous employment and exploitation
- adequate nutrition
- free compulsory primary education
- adequate healthcare
- equal treatment regardless of gender, race or cultural background
- the right to express opinions and freedom of thought in matters affecting them
- safe exposure/access to leisure, play, culture and art.

All of these goals are expressed with respect to the child's age and maturity, and the child's best interests are always the paramount concern. (Adapted from text on a Unicef website, at www.unicefusa.org/infoactiv/rights.html)

The Convention was ratified by the UK government in 1991 and the articles which are most important for protecting the rights of disabled children are:

- **Article 2** – All rights apply to all children equally whatever their race, sex, religion, disability, opinion or family background.
- **Article 6** – Children have a right to life and to the best possible chance to develop fully.
- **Article 23** – Disabled children must be helped to be as independent as possible and to take a full and active part in everyday life.

The Salamanca Statement

In 1994 the United Nations Educational Scientific and Cultural Organisation (Unesco) called on all governments to adopt the principle of inclusive education, enrolling all children in regular schools unless there are compelling reasons for doing otherwise.

UK law and guidance

These are some of the significant legal landmarks for disabled children and their families.

Education Act 1981

This Act was a turning point because it stated that disabled children should be educated in a mainstream school wherever possible. Unfortunately, it allowed significant loopholes. For instance, there were three caveats in place, stating that disabled children could attend mainstream education only if the provision was compatible with:

- the needs of the child
- the needs of other children
- the efficient use of resources.

The 1981 Act also gave local education authorities (LEAs) the duty to:

- assess a child's special educational needs
- issue a statement of those needs
- specify the provision that the authority would make to meet them.

Education Act 1996 (previously 1993)

This Act replaced the 1981 Education Act and was designed to address some of the main areas of difficulty stemming from it. It gave greater rights to parents, duties for schools and firmer procedural rules for the assessment and statementing of children's special educational needs, such as setting time limits for each stage of the process.

The caveats mentioned above in relation to the Education Act 1981 were carried forward under Section 316 of this Act and continued to present a stumbling block for parents wishing for their children to attend mainstream provision as local authorities often excluded disabled children from mainstream education because of one or more of these caveats. The SEN and Disability Act 2001 (see page 34) introduced a new Section 316 into the 1996 Act which changed these conditions. From January 2002, a child with a statement of special educational needs must attend a mainstream school unless that is incompatible with the wishes of the child's parents or the efficient education of other children.

Children Act 1989

This was and is the single most important initiative aimed at improving services for all children. For the first time, the Act included disabled children in the wider framework of legal powers, duties and protections which relate to all children. It states that every local authority should provide services for disabled children in their area so as to minimise the effect of their disability. It emphasises the need for these children to lead lives which are as normal as possible.

Under the Act, social services departments have a general duty to provide day care services and supervised activities for disabled children under five years old and to make provision for school-age children in their out-of-school time. However, this again raises the issue of allocation of limited resources and the reality is that services may be inaccessible, inadequate or offer little choice. This situation continues even though the planning guidance for Early Years Development and Childcare Partnerships reiterates the duty to allocate sufficient places.

Disability Discrimination Act 1995

The Disability Discrimination Act (DDA) brought in new legal measures to clarify disabled people's rights in terms of employment, obtaining goods and services, buying or renting land or property, and transport.

Under the Act, a person is disabled if he or she has a physical or mental impairment which has a substantial and long-term adverse effect on his or her ability to carry out normal day-to-day activities. The term 'physical impairment' includes sensory disability, while 'mental impairment' covers learning disability and mental health problems. An impairment can include a medical condition such as HIV or cancer, emotional or behavioural difficulties or dyslexia, if their adverse effects meet the criterion of being 'substantial and long-term'. The measures laid out in the DDA are aimed at ending the discrimination faced by many disabled children and adults. Employers and those who provide goods and services to the public have to take reasonable steps to ensure that they are not discriminating against disabled people, including children.

The measures covering supply of goods and services applied to providers of social care for young children, and to leisure facilities such as swimming pools and sports centres. Examples of practices which are not legal under this part of the Act include refusing to:

- admit a group of disabled children to a zoo or adventure playground because they are too slow or other visitors might not like it
- rent a property to a family with a disabled child
- let a family with a disabled child sit in a restaurant because the child needs special feeding arrangements
- rent a holiday cottage to a holiday project for young people with learning difficulties. (Russell 1996)

The key duties with respect to the provision of goods and services are that providers of services must not refuse a service, offer a worse standard of service or offer a service on worse terms – unless they can offer a 'justification'. A 'justification' means that providers can take into account health and safety issues, the needs of the child, resources, practicality and/or the interests of other service-users. However, these duties are 'anticipatory', and providers are expected to demonstrate that they are planning ahead to improve access and inclusion.

It would be considered unreasonable in law for providers to have 'blanket' policies to apply to particular 'categories' of disability, for example to assume that all children with diabetes or epilepsy cannot do certain activities.

How the DDA has changed

When the DDA was passed in 1995, education providers (including some early years settings) and local education authorities were exempted from its provisions except as providers of goods and services. This problem has been addressed by the SEN and Disability Act 2001 which removed the exemption of education from the DDA. The Council for Disabled Children and the National Children's Bureau have produced an leaflet that explains what is now required, *Early years and the Disability Discrimination Act. What service providers need to know* (2003).

Part 3 of the DDA covers all providers that are not constituted as schools: day nurseries, family centres, childcare centres, pre-schools, playgroups, individual childminders and networks of accredited childminders and any other private, voluntary and statutory provision that is not established as a school.

Those early years settings that are constituted as schools are covered by Part 4 of the DDA. Part 4 applies to all schools: private or state maintained, mainstream or special. The duties cover discrimination in admissions, the provision of 'education and associated services' and exclusions.

All early years providers will therefore have a duty not to discriminate against disabled pupils in both the education and social care or other services provided.

From September 2002 the DDA requires education providers that are not schools:

- not to treat disabled children 'less favourably' for a reason related to their disability
- to make reasonable adjustments to policies, practices and procedures that make it impossible or unreasonably difficult to make use of a service.

Reasonable adjustments may include auxiliary aids and services and making physical changes (from 2004). In practice, such 'reasonable adjustments' include:

- disability equality training for everyone, with clear policies in risk management, personal care, lifting and handling
- hiring or purchasing portable ramps and other low-cost aids
- ensuring that routine refurbishment plans include arrangements to improve access.

'Reasonable adjustments' for individual children might include:

- training for personal support
- provision of accessible activities in an accessible

environment
- flexibility in terms of toilet arrangements, for example allowing a child to use an accessible staff toilet
- planning flexible transport.

Providers are not required to incur unreasonable expense nor to ignore health and safety considerations, but it should be possible to make short-term adjustments while planning strategically to improve access over time.

The Act raises some tricky issues that should become clearer over time. It is not yet clear for example whether assessment and eligibility criteria could be regarded as discriminatory. Risk assessment and health and safety is another grey area in terms of inclusive practice.

The SEN and Disability Act 2001

Amending the Education Act

Part I of the SEN and Disability Act (SENDA) amended Part IV of the Education Act 1996. Under it, from September 2001 all registered early years providers have been required to have in place the following:

- a written SEN policy
- a designated member of staff who has responsibility for SEN in the setting (the special educational needs coordinator, or SENCO)
- arrangements to participate in relevant training events organised by the LEA and its Early Years Development and Childcare Partnership.

Unregistered providers are required to satisfy the LEA that the first two measures are in place before they can be registered. The Act's planning duties require schools and LEAs to develop accessibility plans and strategies, and to look at how they can best build this planning into individual service and authority-wide planning structures.

The Act has made the following significant changes – only one of the Education Act caveats remains to limit the LEA's duty to provide a mainstream school place for a child with special educational needs (see Education Act 1981, page 29), that is that children with a statement of special educational needs should be included in mainstream schools so long as other children's education is not adversely effected:

- schools must inform parents when they make special education provision because they have identified their child as having special educational needs
- schools may request a statutory assessment in the same way as parents
- new arrangements for amendments to statements
- LEAs are required to provide and advertise parent partnership services
- LEAs are required to make arrangements for resolving disagreements between parents and schools, and between parents and the LEA
- arrangements have been tightened for appeals to the Tribunal, including setting time limits for the implementation of the decisions of the Tribunal.

Amending the Disability Discrimination Act

Part II of the SENDA amended the Disability Discrimination Act 1995 and:

- made it unlawful to discriminate against disabled pupils and prospective pupils

- set out a duty on schools not to treat disabled pupils less favourably than non-disabled pupils
- set out a duty on schools to take reasonable steps to ensure that they don't put disabled pupils at a substantial disadvantage
- provided for remedy through the renamed SEN and Disability Tribunal which will have an extended remit to hear disability discrimination cases
- introduced a duty on LEAs and schools to plan for increased access to schools for disabled pupils
- introduced a power for the Disability Rights Commission (DRC) to prepare codes of practice for providers and others on their new duties. (The DRC is an executive non-departmental public body working to strategic objectives and priorities agreed by the Secretary of State for Education.)

The specific focus of these duties is to protect pupils and potential pupils from discrimination on the grounds of disability, providing us with a legal basis for taking forward the message that disabled adults and children are citizens, consumers and contributors to their local communities.

However the teeth of the legislation may have to be tested before they can provide sufficient bite. There are parallels to be drawn with previous equality legislation such as the Race Relations Act. Things will only change because of hard work and determination. It will not happen overnight.

Human Rights Act 2000

This Act overrides common law and is binding on local authorities. It enshrines in law every individual's right:

- not to be subjected to inhuman treatment
- to a fair hearing

- to respect for home, family and private life
- not to be discriminated against
- to property
- to education.

Article 14 of the Act states that 'the enjoyment of the rights and freedoms shall be secured without discrimination on any ground such as sex, race, colour, language, religion, political or other opinion, national or social origin, associating with a national minority, property, birth or other status'. Disability is covered within that last description: 'other status'.

This Article ensures equality of access to all the rights that are protected in the Act; it cannot be applied on its own. So, the right to go on a school journey may not in itself be regarded as an essential part of the right to education, but preventing a diabetic child from going on school journeys could be unjustified discrimination on the grounds of a disabled child's equal right to education (adapted from Parents for Inclusion 2000).

Care Standards Act 2000

This Act provided for Ofsted to assume responsibility for the regulation of day care and out-of-school care according to minimum standards.

Guidance has been released for all of the different types of early years provision, although many of the criteria to which Ofsted will be inspecting remain the same as those which were previously inspected by local authority social services departments and LEAs.

The guidance is set out under 14 national standards and two annexes, one for babies under two, the other for overnight care.

All of the standards are relevant for disabled children and those with other forms of SEN, but particular attention needs to be paid to:

- Standard 7: health
- Standard 9: equal opportunities
- Standard 10: special needs.

It is important to remember that these are minimum standards, guiding settings in the right direction and helping to ensure a reasonable Ofsted report. However, there is nothing to stop settings and services improving on and adapting practice above and beyond these requirements.

Special Educational Needs Code of Practice 2001

Originally part of the 1996 Education Act, the revised Code of Practice came into force in 2002.

The 1996 Education Act and the Nursery and Grant-Maintained Schools Act 1996 place a duty on all schools and other providers in receipt of the nursery education grant to 'have regard to' the Code of Practice.

The code has very detailed guidance, which you are advised to consult in full (Department for Education and Skills 2001b). In summary, the guidance is informed by the following general principles:

- children with special educational needs should have their needs met
- the special educational needs of children will normally be met in mainstream schools or settings
- the views of children should be sought and taken into account
- parents have a vital role to play in supporting their children's education

- children with special educational needs should be offered full access to a broad and balanced curriculum for the Foundation Stage and the National Curriculum.

The revised code cross-refers to other recent education initiatives such as parent partnership schemes and Sure Start. It emphasises consultation and joint-working, including the involvement of pupils in decisions regarding their own education.

According to the Code of Practice a child has special educational needs if she has a learning difficulty which calls for special educational provision. A child has a learning difficulty if he or she:

1 has a significantly greater difficulty in learning than the majority of children of the same age
2 has a disability which either prevents or hinders him or her from making use of educational facilities of a kind provided for children of the same age in schools within the area of the local education authority
3 is under compulsory school age and falls within the definition at 1 or 2 above, or would do if special educational provision was not made for him or her.

A child *must not* be regarded as having a learning difficulty solely because the language or form of language of the home is different from the language in which he or she will be taught.

This definition includes disabled children as well as children who may have developmental language, learning or behaviour difficulties. The majority of the difficulties that fall under the definition will be mild or transient, but a small percentage of children have such significant needs that they need help from the local authority in the form of an assessment and/or a statement.

New approaches to practice

The eight categories which spelled out different forms of
learning difficulties have been replaced in the new code by
five groups of difficulty:

- communication and interaction
- cognition and learning
- behaviour, emotional and social development
- sensory and/or physical needs
- medical conditions.

The five-stage approach to working with children that was
contained in the old code has now been removed, although
chunks of the original text have survived, particularly on
statementing children with complex needs. With regard to
early years, there are now just two phases for working with
children who require extra help but whose needs have not
been made the subject of a statement:

- Early Years Action
- Early Years Action Plus.

The code says that, where a child's needs are obviously
complex, staff should consider skipping the action stages and
go direct to statementing. There is also new advice on ending
and amending statements, lapsed statements, and when
residential provision might be considered more appropriate
(see page 85 for an explanation of statements and
'statementing').

The code also says that children's progress should be the main
trigger for each new stage of action, and detailed guidance on
this is available in the SEN toolkit document (Department for
Education and Skills 2001c).

Early Years Action

This phase roughly corresponds to stages 1 and 2 of the old code. Triggers for intervention could be practitioners' or parents' concern about a child who, despite receiving appropriate early education:

- makes little or no progress even when teaching approaches are particularly targeted to improve the child's identified area of weakness
- continues working at levels significantly below those expected for children of a similar age in certain areas
- presents persistent emotional and/or behavioural difficulties, which are not ameliorated by the behaviour management techniques usually employed by the setting
- has sensory or physical problems and continues to make little or no progress despite the provision of personal aids and equipment
- has communication and/or interaction difficulties, and requires specific individual interventions in order to access learning.

If practitioners and parents decide that a child needs further support, staff should seek the help of the SENCO (see 'The role of the SENCO', pages 43–46).

The SENCO and colleagues should then collect the following:

- observations and other records relating to the child held by the setting
- up-to-date information from parents (with support, if necessary)
- information held by LEA educational psychologists (with parental consent)
- information held by other relevant external agencies (with parental consent).

If possible, contact should also be made with the LEA's parent partnership officer, who can liaise with parents on all aspects of special educational need.

Any action taken as a result of studying these documents should enable a young child with special educational needs to learn and progress to his or her maximum potential through arrangements tailored specifically for him or her using appropriate resources, including adult time.

Strategies employed to enable the child to progress should be recorded within an individual education plan (IEP). IEPs should be discussed with parents at regular intervals, and kept under continual review. Young children are constantly changing and so it is best practice to review their IEP about every six weeks, and never to leave an interval of longer than three months. The box 'Checklist for IEPs' contains guidance on the information that should be included in an IEP.

Checklist for IEPs

- Date on which the IEP was compiled.
- Name of the provision.
- Child's name.
- Child's date of birth and current age.
- Stage of professional intervention in terms of the Code of Practice (for example Early Years Action).
- Overall goals for the child which reflect his or her perceived difficulties.
- Specific targets appropriate for the child.
- Methods, activities and resources that will best enable the child.
- Members of staff responsible for input.
- Frequency, duration and location of appropriate input.
- Method of recording progress.
- Specific comments or advice from parent.
- Proposed review date.

It is useful to attach any other appropriate records to the IEP.

Early Years Action Plus

This phase of intervention is characterised by the involvement of external support services. The triggers for referral could be that, despite Early Years Action measures, the child:

- continues to make little or no progress in specific areas over a long period
- continues working at an early years curriculum substantially below that expected of children at a similar age
- has emotional or behavioural difficulties which substantially and regularly interfere with the child's own learning or that of the group
- has additional sensory or physical needs and/or requires specialist intervention
- has ongoing communication or interaction difficulties that impede social development or learning.

If intervention fails, statutory assessment should be sought with a view to the provision of a Statement of Special Educational Need (see page 85).

The role of the SENCO

The importance of having a special educational needs coordinator (SENCO) in every early years setting has been stated clearly in government guidance. The EYDCP planning guidance 2001–2002 (Department for Education and Skills 2001a) says that: 'As a minimum, the implementation Plan should show intended progress towards ensuring that every early years setting has identified a SENCO with responsibility for SEN (para. 3.26)', and 'During 2001–2002 Partnerships should have defined clearly the role and objectives for area SENCOs (para 3.37)'.

The Code of Practice goes even further, saying that:

> Provision for children with special educational needs is a matter for everyone in the setting. In addition to the setting's head teacher or manager and the SEN coordinator (SENCO) all other members of staff have important responsibilities. In practice, the division of day-to-day responsibilities is a matter for individual settings. (Department for Education and Skills 2001b)

The main responsibility of a setting-based SENCO is for the everyday operation of SEN policy and this may include:

- ensuring that the setting establishes appropriate procedures in relation to working with and including disabled children and those with other forms of SEN
- working with other staff and parents on producing a written SEN policy
- ensuring that the SEN policy cross-refers effectively with other relevant policies (admissions, equal opportunities, etc.)
- monitoring and reviewing the SEN policy.

In addition, SENCOs are responsible for coordinating provision for children with SEN within their setting. This may include ensuring that:

- the needs of disabled children and those with other forms of SEN are being included in all aspects of the setting's planning and practice
- all staff have an understanding of the setting's practice in relation to disabled children and those with other forms of SEN, and that there is consistency and continuity in the way it is carried out.

Although not specified in the Code of Practice, we recommend that a SENCO should also be responsible for maintaining an SEN register or equivalent recording system. This system could usefully include the names of all children in the setting identified as having SEN, the stage of the Code of Practice at which each child is currently placed and the date of the next review of the IEP. They should also monitor the register, updating the names, stages and next review date as appropriate.

The SENCO should also:

- coordinate and keep on file all information and correspondence on children with SEN, and ensure appropriate access to it
- ensure that records are kept for each individual child
- support staff in making observations, and set appropriate targets for meeting individual children's needs and entitlements by ensuring that appropriate Individual Education Plans are in place
- contribute to formal assessments and reviews for children who have statements (see Chapter 6 for more on assessments and statements).

Other SENCO duties

1 **Liaising with parents of children with SEN** – SENCOs have an important role in developing and maintaining positive relationships in order to ensure effective liaison with parents. Although it may not be the SENCO's direct responsibility to liaise with every individual parent or carer of a child with SEN, she must ensure that it happens as constructively and effectively as possible. The SENCO should also be responsible for supporting staff in meetings or reviews with parents, and in setting appropriate targets, review dates and times. (For more on working with parents, see Chapter 7.)
2 **Contributing to in-service training** – The SENCO can make a significant contribution to staff professional development by keeping up to date with any national or local developments on provision for children with SEN, ensuring that the relevant

information is effectively passed on to staff and management, and identifying and addressing the individual training needs of staff in relation to SEN and disability.

3 **Liaising with external agencies** – The SENCO should take responsibility for the setting's liaison with external agencies, including the local authority educational psychology service, to gain information, advice or support in relation to disability and SEN issues.

There are advantages and disadvantages to having only one member of staff who carries these responsibilities. The main advantage is that at least one person in every setting has a lead responsibility for special educational needs. The disadvantage is that other members of staff may not accept responsibility for being sympathetic to, or knowledgeable about, an individual child's requirements. The ideal situation, and a goal worth aspiring to, is where all members of staff have sufficient knowledge and understanding of any child's special educational needs, though this will be more manageable in a small playgroup with two or three staff members than in larger settings.

Equal opportunities

The EYDCP planning guidance 2001–2002 says:

> As part of …[the equal opportunities strategy], early years settings should identify and train someone to take responsibility for establishing and implementing the setting's equal opportunities strategy. In most cases this is likely to be the setting-based SENCO. (Department for Education and Skills 2001a, para. 2.58)

Some providers, however, may find it more effective to appoint an equal opportunities coordinator with a specific role and responsibilities.

4 Developing inclusive policies

The special educational needs policy needs to identify the process for a change of ethos, the barriers that currently prevent inclusion and what needs to be done to remove those barriers.

Richard Rieser (Alliance for Inclusive Education)

Deciding to admit all children into mainstream education, and ensuring that they can attend, is only a small part of the process of inclusion. Children will not really belong to a group unless the hearts and minds of those involved are convinced that this is a positive way forward. We need to look at policy-making as a functional tool, and not just a set of rules and requirements.

Since 2001/02, early years providers in receipt of the nursery education grant *must* have a special educational needs policy. Planning and implementing an SEN policy is an opportunity for practitioners, parents and children to focus on the 'how' and 'why' of including disabled children and to air any doubts, fears or even hostility and misunderstanding of the process. Potential problems and difficulties should be aired at the outset. Some of these may be valid and should be taken seriously.

It is important to include in the policy-making process representatives from all the groups who are involved, however peripherally. Indeed, the revised Code of Practice strongly emphasises the importance of teamwork, and the empowerment and participation of parents and children. (For a description of the Code, see pages 38–43.)

Before attempting to draw up inclusive policies, it is vital to give proper consideration to the points listed in the box 'Issues for inclusive provision' (see below). An inability to meet some of these requirements should not be regarded as a barrier to starting the process of inclusion. However, the areas of provision listed are important and, where possible, the requirements should be met. Some excellent groups and nurseries have developed fully inclusive provision in circumstances that were far from ideal, such as having difficult staircases to negotiate.

If your setting is planning an SEN policy or a policy on inclusion, training for practitioners on disability equality and inclusion can provide an invaluable backdrop to the policy-making process. It offers staff the opportunity to develop an understanding of the issues involved, and to reflect on the implications for good practice.

Making a policy on inclusion

A policy is a statement of the beliefs, values and goals of an organisation that ensures consistency in practice across the whole organisation. Individual children may have very different needs which must be met on an individual basis. A policy should give a common message to practitioners, parents, children and anyone else who comes into contact with the setting or service. It should broaden their horizons and help them to share good practice. Procedures may be outlined in a policy or may be developed afterwards; they are the policy in action.

There are several stages in making a policy and the written document should reflect these stages.

Issues for inclusive provision

Any setting that intends to be inclusive needs to consider the following aspects of provision in relation to all the children in its care, and adapt procedures accordingly so that disabled children can participate fully alongside their non-disabled peers.

An inclusive setting:

- provides access to the environment
- provides access to the curriculum
- provides access to physical activities
- provides access to outings
- considers access to transport
- includes disability issues in the curriculum
- ensures curriculum diversity
- provides effective learning support through appropriate support staff
- regards and uses sign language as a mother tongue
- uses inclusive communication such as large print, Braille and audiotape
- uses videos with subtitles and/or British Sign Language
- uses pictorial symbols, where useful
- has a policy on administering medication
- maintains equipment, including special equipment
- encourages and promotes children's participation
- encourages and promotes partnership with parents, including disabled parents
- provides role models
- provides training in disability equality and awareness for practitioners and management committee members or governors.

(Adapted from Reiser and Mason 1992)

Mission statement

This is a statement of intentions. It should reflect the desires of all service-users and identify what they wish to happen, regardless of costs or resources. The mission statement does not need to be long; a few short sentences will usually be sufficient to describe the principles of your service. If it is easier, you could brainstorm key words or phrases that reflect your policy aspirations in a staff meeting, and arrange them formally into a statement later on.

Before writing the mission statement, it can be helpful to first clarify what inclusion means in the context of your setting and environment, and to adopt a working definition.

> ### Sample mission statement
>
> At Anansi, we believe that all children have a right to a warm, loving, caring, safe and stimulating environment which respects the diversity of cultures and individuality. We want our centre to be inclusive and child-centred, where children of all abilities can participate fully in decision-making and learning, and having fun.
>
> Anansi Nursery, Harlesden

Statement of reasons

This is a statement of why it is important for the setting's policy on inclusion to follow the principles laid out in the mission statement. An effective way to include the views of practitioners, parents and children in the statement of reasons is to ask everyone some open-ended questions about how to provide an inclusive service (see box below), and to use their answers when devising the text for that statement.

Questions to help devise a statement of reasons

- What is disability?
- What is my experience of disability?
- Is society afraid of disability? Why?
- Am I afraid of disability? Why?
- Do we, as a society, treat disabled children as individuals in their own right?
- Do we enable them to have access to equal opportunities with other children?
- What do disabled children and adults think about disability?
- What support do disabled children need?
- How can we provide them with that support?
- What support is needed by non-disabled parents to help them understand disability?
- What structural changes are needed in our setting/service (environment, institutions, training, etc.)?
- How does society need to change our feelings, attitudes and practices regarding disabled children and adults? What can I do?
- How can we promote a different view of disability within our society? What can I do?

(Adapted from Cameron and Sturge Moore 1990)

Practice audit

The practice audit allows you to gather information about how inclusive your setting or service is at the moment. The audit should be designed to answer the following questions:

- Are any disabled children using the service now?
- Is the environment inclusive? (See page 21 for a definition of inclusive education.)

- Are the activities offered inclusive?
- What are the service's strengths and weaknesses?
- What special equipment, staff and adaptations does the service offer to support disabled children?
- What steps do we take in our setting to involve children in decision-making and planning?
- Have we taken the needs of disabled children into account when establishing procedures to deal with new initiatives such as the Foundation Stage Profile and the National Literacy Strategy?

Goals

It is important to set short achievable goals (for example reviewing the setting's prospectus), as well as long-term ones (for example securing funding for staff team training).

The policy document

There is no particular formula to writing an SEN/inclusion policy, but an inclusive policy document could include sections on:

- your mission statement
- the aims and objectives of the SEN/inclusion policy
- the name of the SENCO
- a description of the role of the SENCO
- admission arrangements for children with SEN
- any specialist facilities and/or specialisms your setting has to offer
- any additional resources for children with SEN and how they are allocated
- the process of identification and assessment for children with SEN, and who is responsible

- how the setting has regard to the Code of Practice
- how the setting has adopted the Early Years Action/Action Plus model, and who carries responsibility for its implementation
- how the early years curriculum is planned to make access to the Foundation Stage as full as possible
- how the learning environment provides opportunities for children to be included in the setting as a whole
- how you have consulted the stakeholders (parents, children, staff) on the SEN/inclusion policy
- how you will disseminate the SEN/inclusion policy
- how you will monitor, evaluate and review the SEN/inclusion policy including timescales
- how you will deal with complaints about the SEN/inclusion policy
- your staffing policy in relation to children with SEN
- how you work with external professionals and agencies, and who they are
- your staff training policy on SEN
- how you work in partnership with parents
- your links with schools, childminding networks and other early years settings
- your links with other support services and agencies.

A framework like this can help ensure that you meet the requirements and have addressed all the policy issues. It is important to make the policy document easy to read and understand.

The following points may be useful:

- layout should be clear
- unavoidable jargon or acronyms should be explained
- sections should be set out in a logical sequence
- the main messages should be highlighted by bold text or the use of boxes.

It is important for everyone to have access to the policy document and for them to understand it. Be aware of different needs and be ready to make the policy available in different formats, such as large print, audiotape or Braille. Local associations for blind people should be able to offer help and advice regarding Braille and audiotape recording. A good photocopier will enlarge print adequately (providing the original print is clear and dark).

It may be useful to prepare a brief leaflet summarising the policy which can be given to anyone in contact with the service. Put the mission statement on display, on notice-boards for instance, and include it in your prospectus.

Good practice checklists

These good practice checklists are intended to raise issues and stimulate thinking on the range of ways in which your service can ensure equality for disabled children and adults. They are adapted from *Equal opportunities: a guide to ensuring good practice on disability in UK fieldwork* (Save the Children 1992).

It may be helpful to work through the checklists with your colleagues to agree which items raise relevant issues and what action you would like to take on them.

Many of the suggestions are fairly simple and low-cost, others are things to aim towards. We do not live in an ideal world and we may never be able to tackle some of the resource issues, but the most important thing is to acknowledge disabled children's and adults' rights and to look for ways to make them a reality.

Staff

Do the staff and management in your setting have:

- A commitment to anti-discriminatory practice and an equality approach?
- A shared responsibility to address these matters in a consistent manner?
- An equally high expectation of staff and all service-users?
- The confidence and opportunity to discuss together issues that may arise relating to disability?

Ensuring access (physical, materials and communication)

Have the staff and management in your setting:

- A shared understanding of the concept of access?
- Identified any low-cost changes that can be made in the next year to improve access and arrangements?
- Consulted with any disabled users of buildings (staff, children, parents, carers) about any small changes to arrangements which might be helpful?
- Ensured the display of materials that reflect a positive image of disabled people and children?
- Produced accessible information, for example leaflets, posters in large print?
- An agreed approach to terminology?

Children and parents/carers

Do the staff and management in your setting:

- Encourage all the children to develop a positive sense of self-image and a pride in their own identity?
- Encourage disabled children to accept challenge and participate in a wide range of activities?

- Have equally high expectations of all children and take steps to ensure that they can take sensible risks?
- Hold full information about individual children's health care needs?
- Foster within all children the responsibility of accepting and valuing others as they are?
- Challenge any bullying or discriminatory behaviour that may occur around disability issues?
- Know where to get information, guidance and support when necessary?
- Have links with community professionals for direct help in training in relation to care needed by individual children?

5 Play and learning in an inclusive setting

Curriculum guidance for the Foundation Stage

The Foundation Stage begins when children reach the age of three – at a time when most of them are attending, or starting to attend, some form of pre-school or nursery provision – and finishes at the end of the reception year.

The curriculum guidance describes the step-by-step approach to early learning goals in six areas of learning:

- personal, social and emotional development
- communication, language and literacy
- mathematical development
- knowledge and understanding of the world
- physical development
- creative development.

(Department for Education and Employment and Qualifications and Curriculum Authority 2000)

The early learning goals replaced the desirable learning outcomes, which were previously used to assess young children's progress. The Foundation Stage applies to all settings in receipt of nursery education grant funding, and schools with nursery- and reception-aged children in England. The guidance is unusual in that it represents a true collaboration with experts in the sector and is to be celebrated for the consensus that it has achieved. We now have a document which represents the first steps towards a unified approach based on common principles and language which all our children deserve. It is an essential tool for early years practitioners and managers, and complements the early learning goals, which are not intended as 'stand alone' targets in isolation from the guidance.

The principal aim of the guidance is to help practitioners plan how their work will contribute to the achievement of the early learning goals. It is designed to be effective and useful in the full range of settings where three to five year olds are found. It is based on the premise that all children should be given the opportunity to experience the very best possible start to their education, and seeks to support the development of early communication, literacy and numeracy skills that will prepare young children for Key Stage 1 of the National Curriculum. It also stresses that the curriculum for the Foundation Stage should underpin all future learning by supporting, fostering and developing children's:

- personal, social and emotional wellbeing
- positive attitudes and dispositions towards their learning
- social skills and attention skills
- persistence.

The early learning goals establish expectations for most children to reach by the end of the Foundation Stage, but they are not a curriculum in themselves. The guidance sets out in detail the practical and illustrative examples of what might reasonably be expected of different children at different stages in the Foundation Stage. There is a stepping-stones approach which outlines how a child from age three may progress towards each goal, and is intended to help practitioners identify developmentally appropriate activities. There are also examples of what children can do and what the practitioner needs to do.

Partnership with parents and other key adult professionals is stressed as an integral part of building on the learning that children bring with them to settings. Most children are expected to achieve the early learning goals by the end of the Foundation Stage.

Principles for early years education

The Foundation Stage curriculum guidance sets out fundamental principles for quality early education, along with practical advice and examples of good practice in a range of settings. These principles are:

- Effective education requires both a relevant curriculum and practitioners who understand and are able to implement the curriculum requirements.
- Effective education requires practitioners who understand that children develop rapidly during the early years – physically, intellectually, emotionally and socially.
- Practitioners must ensure that all children feel included, secure and valued.
- Early years experience should build on what children already know and can do.
- No child should be excluded or disadvantaged because of ethnicity, culture or religion, home language, family background, special educational needs, disability, gender or ability.
- Parents and practitioners should work together in an atmosphere of mutual respect within which children can have security and confidence.
- To be effective, an early years curriculum should be carefully structured.
- There should be opportunities for children to engage in activities planned by adults and also those that they plan or

initiate themselves.

- Practitioners must be able to observe and respond appropriately to children.
- Well-planned, purposeful activity and appropriate intervention by practitioners will engage children in the learning process and help them make progress in their learning.
- For children to have rich and stimulating experiences, the learning environment should be well planned and well organised.
- Above all, effective learning and development for young children requires high-quality care and education by practitioners.

Taken together, these principles constitute an impressively inclusive approach, though turning the rhetoric into reality can be a demanding as well as rewarding process.

Meeting the diverse needs of children

The guidance emphasises that an awareness and understanding of the requirements of equal opportunities is essential. Specific guidance is given regarding:

- children with special educational need and disabilities
- children with English as an additional language
- learning and teaching
- play.

The section on children with SEN and other disabilities recognises the importance of appropriate support and the need to aid children's understanding through the use of all available senses and experiences (Department for Education and Employment and Qualifications and Curriculum Authority 2000). The section on children with English as an additional language stresses the need to value linguistic diversity, and to build on 'children's experiences of language at home and in the wider community by providing a range of opportunities to use their home language so that their developing use of English and other languages support one another'. Meanwhile, play is officially recognised as a way in which children can 'explore, develop and represent learning experiences that can help them make sense of the world'.

Inclusive practice and the curriculum

Despite the care taken in the Foundation Stage curriculum guidance to ensure that the early learning goals are viewed as broad expectations, there is a risk that uninformed practitioners may regard them as attainment targets, leading them to devalue the achievements of children who 'fail' to meet the goals by the end of the reception year. The guidance acknowledges positive self-esteem as a fundamental prerequisite for successful learning, and we must guard against attitudes which only value children's achievements in narrow and prescriptive terms.

For disabled children, it is particularly important that we value each small but important step. Wherever possible, our aim should be to make the usual range of play and learning opportunities offered by early years services accessible to disabled children. Having 'special' activities for the 'special' children and buying lots of expensive 'special needs' equipment does not help the development of inclusive services. Those seeking to create an educational environment aimed at meeting the entitlements of *all* children should take into account the following suggestions that are vital to curriculum planning and implementation for children with SEN:

- identify and plan appropriately to meet individual needs, using all the available information, including that from parents
- provide a well-planned and structured environment with access for all children
- provide a range of activities, resources and equipment, and be creative in adapting them
- provide access to different types and levels of interaction and communication
- make use of all available specialist skills and strategies
- record individual learning and achievements and evaluate them positively
- ensure all children have access to the six areas of learning in the early learning goals.

All children have the right to a curriculum that is appropriate to their needs. An enabling practitioner will gain as much information as possible about children in her care, but also meet them on their own terms as unique individuals.

Ruth Wilson makes the following observations:

> For the young child with special educational needs, it is critical to consider that the nature of a disability can interfere with his or her experience of the environment as it is presented or arranged by the classroom teacher. This interference tends to diminish the child's learning opportunities in the classroom. Educators therefore cannot assume that the needs of every child can be met by creating a stimulating classroom environment and encouraging children to 'learn on their own'. No matter how enriching the environment appears to be, it is not enriching to the child who cannot access it for one reason or another.
> (Wilson 1998)

Wilson recommends individualised objectives for children based on a developmental approach to the curriculum. She believes that the criteria for objectives which reflect developmentally appropriate practice should:

- be written broadly to allow for flexibility
- allow implementation within the context of the daily routine
- include skills that will increase opportunities for positive interactions with typically developing peers
- represent child-initiated versus teacher-directed behaviours
- be appropriate to the child's developmental level
- allow for generalisation across settings and activities
- reflect current competencies as well as areas of concern
- serve a functional purpose
- include skills that will increase options for successful participation in future inclusive environments.

(Wilson 1998)

Making activities inclusive

Early years practitioners are often concerned because an individual child does not 'fit in' to a particular framework of activity. Some children are even excluded from groups because of difficulties, such as challenging behaviour during circle time or story time. Early years practitioners must question their own rigidity in such matters. Is circle time always necessary? Does it happen for organisational reasons as much as for the benefit of the children? Perhaps a more flexible arrangement which offers other activities alongside circle time might be more appropriate. Changes in routine, arising from the needs of a particular child, can benefit the whole group.

The temptation to do things for a disabled child should be resisted. It is often possible to adapt a game or activity so that it is appropriate in terms of what the child can do him or herself, and allows him or her to be genuinely creative.

Bearing this in mind, it is worth spending some time looking at your service, and thinking about how flexibility and adaptation can be built in:

- What is the environment like?
- What do we offer?
- What is it like to be a child in our service?
- How can we change the environment/programme/working practices to make our service more inclusive?

The information in the rest of this chapter will inform your thoughts on these issues. Do not worry if suggestions here seem too much to do at once, as it would be inappropriate to do so anyway. The best way to develop inclusive provision is to consider the needs of individual children in your service and build up your resources to meet those needs.

Environments, activities and equipment for inclusive play

The outdoor environment

Are there quiet, sheltered areas as well as space for ball games and for wheeled toys to move around safely?

If there is a garden area, does it stimulate all the senses? Here are some ideas for doing so.

- **Sound** – wind chimes; plants and feeders to encourage birds; grasses and other plants whose leaves will rustle in the wind; a fountain or running water.
- **Touch** – different surfaces to walk/ride on; plants with furry leaves, smooth leaves, pine cones, berries (non-poisonous).

- **Smell** – pots with growing herbs; plants with scented flowers or leaves.
- **Taste** – a kitchen garden growing fruit and vegetables, especially those which can be eaten raw so they still look much as they did when they were growing.
- **Sight** – flowers planted so that there is good contrast, for example a bright flower against a dark foliage shrub, or blocks of flowers of one colour.

Grounds for sharing (Stoneham 1996), a guide to developing the grounds of special schools, contains many more ideas which could be used by early years services.

Wheeled toys

A suitable range of wheeled toys might be:

- 'trundle' trikes, which do not need pedalling
- carts which can be towed by children or trikes
- hand-propelled trikes
- tricycles with support seats and lap belts
- a car (either pedal or push-along) with a roof, which will give visually impaired children more confidence.

Fixed playground equipment

If you have fixed playground equipment, try to provide:

- a range of support seats for swings
- various ways of getting on to the equipment, for example a ramp or shallow steps
- wide slides so that two children, or a child and an adult, can slide down together
- hand-rails (in a contrasting colour) where they are needed
- rubber safety surfacing, which is easier than bark to walk on and manoeuvre a wheelchair

- white strips on the edges of platforms and steps.

For a detailed discussion of how to make the best use of outdoor areas, and what to do if you do not have one, see Ouvry 2000.

The indoor environment

It is worth considering whether some of the following modifications might be useful for individual children, and the group as a whole.

- Provide tables with adjustable height, or a range of tables of different heights.
- Provide sand and water trays that can be placed on the floor as well as on a stand.
- Arrange furniture so that there is plenty of space to move around.
- Put symbols or pictures on cupboard doors and entrances to rooms, to indicate what equipment or activities are inside.
- Have a range of beanbags, cushions and mattresses that will help to position children.
- Encourage children and staff to leave furniture in the same place. Always close cupboard doors and keep passageways clear of clutter, to encourage visually impaired children to explore with confidence.
- Avoid shiny surfaces (tables, floors) and provide methods for controlling the amount of light (adjustable window blinds, dimmer switches, angle-poise lights) so that partially sighted children can make the best use of their vision.
- Improve the acoustics, using soft furnishings, and try to keep background noise to a minimum. Provide a quiet area where children who use hearing aids can practise their listening skills (hearing aids amplify all noises, not just those that the child wishes to concentrate on).

Communication

There are several steps you can take to improve communication in your group.

- Familiarise yourself with communication systems used by disabled people – signing, picture symbols or Braille, for example – starting with systems which are relevant to children in your service. Use them when telling stories, singing songs and saying rhymes and in visual displays. Made-up games will help encourage all children to use them.
- Be aware of your body language and facial expressions, and how they can be used to get your message across.
- Make sure that light (either artificial or natural) falls on your face, so that children can see your lip movements and facial expressions easily.
- Before asking a question or asking a child to do something, always say that child's name first, so all the children can relax and only attend to comments addressed to them.

Encouraging interaction between the children

Young children will recognise difference but will not usually put a value to difference unless adults give them this message. You may have to explain why a child with autism or severe learning disabilities, for example, does not conform to standards of behaviour expected of the other children – why he may refuse to sit at the table, bite, scratch or pull hair. Try to explain that the child is unable to understand what is being said, or what behaviour is expected, and therefore becomes frustrated and angry. It is important to help children understand that biting or hair-pulling from this particular child is not an attack on them personally, but a response to a situation he feels unable to control or understand.

If you have to explain to other children why one child cannot do a particular thing, make sure that you also highlight the things the child can do.

Encourage a general atmosphere in which all children help each other, where a disabled child can offer help to non-disabled children, and non-disabled children offer help without 'mothering' disabled children.

Storytelling

There are techniques that help to make stories accessible to all children.

- Use visual props – magnetic board, flannelgraph (a kind of big fuzzy felt board), toys, empty bubble-bath containers (for example Bob the Builder) – to make the story more real to children who have a visual or hearing impairment, or who have difficulty understanding the story.
- Use stories which involve the children in doing actions, giving responses, shouting out repeated phrases, and so on.
- Use puppets, taped sounds and dressing-up clothes which are easy to put on, such as scarves, hats and shawls.
- Use signing (Makaton or British Sign Language), facial expression and gestures.
- Have a range of dual language books with British Sign Language, Makaton, Bliss or Braille. (The different languages are described in 'Books for young children', page 75.)

Games

Games can be for everyone if you make a few simple changes.

- Adapt the rules to cater for varying abilities, for example 'football' can be played by all the children sitting on the floor and hitting the ball with their hands or feet.

- Involve the children in adapting a game so that everyone can take part.
- It may help to use bigger bats than usual for a particular game, or to choose a different kind of ball, for instance:
  - heavier balls that roll slowly
  - balls that are weighted so that they roll eccentrically
  - balls with bells inside
  - balloons instead of balls
  - Koosh balls, made with hundreds of rubber strands sticking out from the centre, that don't bounce or roll out of reach.
- Look for cooperative games, such as parachute games, rather than competitive ones.

Art and craft

All of the following activities can be appreciated by any young child, and children with limited means of expression will especially benefit from them.

- Wrap foam padding or foam-pipe cladding round the handles of paintbrushes, to make them easier to hold.
- Use large decorating rollers and household paintbrushes.
- Use long-handled rollers (used for painting behind radiators), to help children reach further.
- Mix sand in paint to add texture for finger painting.
- Give each colour of paint a different smell, using food essences and perfumes. Do something similar with playdough.
- Introduce different textures and smells into collage work.
- Use large pieces of paper to encourage children to paint together.
- Provide different surfaces to paint on – easel, table, wall, floor.

- Encourage children to paint outside brick walls and paving stones with water and mud.
- Draw round children and fill in the outline with collage or paint.
- Mix cornflour and water for a wonderful sensory experience.

Music

Music has the capacity to reach children who have difficulty responding to other activities.

- Look for instruments which vibrate, such as a guitar or wooden tongue drum, so that hearing-impaired children can feel them.
- Hang instruments up so that they can be hit with one hand.
- Attach a cord to a hanging instrument, such as wind chimes or bells, and to the child's wrist or foot, so that they make a sound when they move.
- Use action songs and signing.
- Use appropriate music for relaxation sessions.

Table toys and large activity equipment

Encourage children to explore equipment and activities by using a variety of ideas for table toys.

- Anchor toys to the table, using Dycem (a non-slip plastic material) and magnetic tape, or by attaching an extended wooden base to the toy which can be clamped to the table.
- Replace small knobs on inset boards with larger knobs or plastic golf tees.
- Make games which reflect the children's experiences, for example transport matching games can include wheelchairs,

make photo games and jigsaws using photographs of the children in the group.

- Make matching games using textures, shapes or smells instead of pictures.
- Make simple sound lotto games.
- Make feely-bag games.

Facilities such as soft play rooms, ball pools and inflatable air mattresses can help to develop social skills as well as physical strength and coordination. They can also help to build the confidence of children who have difficulty moving around or who have a visual impairment.

Multi-sensory environments and sensory banks

Many disabled children may need help to use their senses effectively, to make best use of the sight they have, perhaps, or develop their sense of touch. But a sensory curriculum will benefit all young children.

A sensory bank can be set up gradually and at relatively low cost. An individual staff member might take responsibility for providing activities to stimulate a particular sense, and then rotate the senses around between staff members. Further information on setting up and using a sensory bank is available in *A Sensory Curriculum for Very Special People* (Longhorn 1995)

Simple multi-sensory environments can be set up in a corner of any room which has curtains or blinds to exclude natural light. Shine coloured torches or spotlights onto lengths of muslin or net curtaining, hang faceted or mirrored Christmas baubles in the beam of light and set them gently spinning to produce the same effect as mirror balls in discos. Play gentle music and recordings of waves, whales or bird song and use aromatherapy oils or incense to create a relaxing environment. Introduce various textures to explore and look for cheap toys which incorporate lights, sounds or vibration.

Choosing play and education equipment

There are various potential sources from which to find the right equipment. General guidance is given here. See Appendix 3 for a list of useful suppliers of equipment for inclusive play and education.

Mass market toys

Mass market toys designed for non-disabled children are often suitable for some disabled children, possibly with simple adaptations. They are relatively cheap and they have the advantage of being appealing to children, which is important in an inclusive service.

Educational catalogues

Educational catalogues include some of the mass market toys, plus others with a more educational emphasis. Most catalogues have equipment suitable for disabled children, and some make a special highlight of them.

Special needs suppliers

A few special needs suppliers produce play and leisure equipment specifically for disabled people. The equipment is always expensive and not necessarily of good quality, but the main problem is that most of it looks different from and more boring than other toys – which is not good for inclusion. Many of the most expensive items are very focused, in that they only do one thing and do not encourage children to develop a range of activities. Look for equipment which is suitable for a wide range of abilities and which will be enjoyed by both disabled and non-disabled children; Edu-play and Tocki are particularly good at this (see Appendix 3).

DIY equipment

Many very successful pieces of equipment can be made by early years practitioners, parents or volunteers. Often you can see what the child needs but there is nothing suitable in the catalogues, so the answer is to make it. There are several books (for example Lear 1996) which are full of simple ideas for DIY toys, to get you started. We are not talking here about making exact copies of commercial products, that is rarely successful and your time is usually better spent talking to local charities or community groups who might be willing to purchase the item for you.

Positive images of disabled people

Images of disabled people are rare in any form of media, whether it be posters, books, films or television. And if they are present, they are very negative. Typical images show disabled people as pitiable and pathetic, sinister or evil, laughable, victims, or incapable of fully participating in everyday lives. Portraying disabled people as invisible or one-dimensional reinforces the discrimination and isolation disabled people experience in all aspects of life.

Most children and young people have little contact with disabled people, and their views are strongly influenced by the media. This is why it is so important to ensure that we provide positive images of disability for young children, both in their playthings and in the visual images that surround them.

Although it is important to recognise high achievers in any field, it is not helpful to emphasise images of 'super cripples', such as wheelchair racers in the London Marathon or athletes in the Paralympics. Most disabled people simply want to be shown participating fully in everyday life, as students, workers, consumers (do you see disabled people in advertisements or mail order catalogues?), parents, travellers and so on.

We live in a multicultural society and we expect our children's playthings to reflect that fact. More than six million disabled people are part of our society too, but there are few images of disability to be found. Dolls and other model figures are invariably 'perfect', unless they are 'baddies' or specific examples of character merchandising, such as Disney's Hunchback of Notre Dame.

Children's books rarely include disabled children or adults as part of the story or pictures; they are sometimes the focus of the story, but are more often completely absent. Here are some resources with positive, everyday images of disabled people. See Appendix 3 for the listed suppliers.

Jigsaws

The 'Everyday Life' and 'Our Children' sets of photographic jigsaws produced by NES Arnold include children with disabilities. A simple wooden face jigsaw showing a girl wearing spectacles is available from Rede Hobbies.

Games

To date, there are no games for young children which include images of disability. It is possible to make various picture-matching games using photographs, pictures cut from catalogues or drawings. For example, a picture lotto on the theme of transport could include pictures of wheelchairs.

Books for young children

Look for books which include a disabled child or adult as part of the story, but with no reference to the disability. Other books focus more on disability, which may be acceptable provided this is done in a positive way.

Two good sources of children's books which reflect an anti-discriminatory approach are Community Insight and Letterbox Library.

Many disabled people use alternative communication systems to support or replace spoken or written language.

- Hearing-impaired children may use British Sign Language (an independent visual language which has its own grammar) or Signed English, which is intended for use at the same time as spoken English and uses signs and finger spelling to give an exact representation of spoken English.
- Children with learning disabilities may use Makaton, a simpler sign language which also has symbols to support text.
- Blind children may use Braille, a system of raised dots in which each letter is represented by a different pattern of dots and the text is read by touch.
- Blissymbolics is a symbol system used by many children who are unable to make the precise hand movements required by sign language.

Children's books which incorporate these communication systems will help non-disabled children learn about different forms of communication and contribute to the overall impression that the setting welcomes all children.

Books which include sign language and finger spelling are available from the Forest Bookshop, by mail order. Some books with Blissymbols are available from Blissymbol Communication (UK). English/Braille books are produced by ClearVision, who operate a loan system. Books are adapted by sticking Braille strips onto the pages or by interleaving clear plastic pages of Braille.

Posters

Because of the shortage of visual images of disability, it is sometimes tempting to use posters which, on more careful consideration, do not give positive messages. Many of the posters available are not positive and few are suitable for early years settings.

Contact Action for Leisure for further information on play materials, books and posters which show positive images of disability.

Disability toys

Some educational suppliers have wheelchairs and other items for use with dolls. These are invariably expensive and will be of limited value if used in isolation.

Research carried out by Save the Children raised concerns about the effectiveness of 'disability toys' and showed a contrast in how the toys were used by different groups of children (Pettit and Laws 1997). Children who had some experience of disability (usually because they had a disabled relative) would make appropriate use of the dolls and their equipment (wheelchair, crutches and hearing aid) and relate them to their own experience. But children who had little knowledge of disability tended to use the wheelchair as a roller skate, the crutches as guns and identify the hearing aid as a Walkman. If they mentioned disability, they seemed to equate it with illness and with temporary disability, such as a broken leg, from which the doll would recover.

This suggests that simply placing a doll in a wheelchair in the home corner is unlikely to contribute to an increase in the children's awareness and appreciation of diversity. The disability toys, and disabled dolls in particular, need a context if they are to be successful.

That said, the Little Tikes playhouse has a wheelchair and ramp available which encourages positive play and learning because it is part of a wider imaginative setting.

The following guidelines will help you create a context for disability dolls that will help all children learn and benefit from its presence.

- Encourage discussion and exploration:
  - If you have a whole selection of dolls, ask the children if one of them is disabled.
  - How can they ensure that the disabled doll can join in all the other dolls' activities?
  - How can the doll be kept safe while taking part? (Perhaps talk about seat-belts in cars and lap belts in wheelchairs, make a lap-belt using ribbon or string.)
  - How can the disabled doll access other parts of the house, especially upstairs? Talk about, and look at pictures, of stair lifts; maybe visit a house which has a stair lift.
- Choose a book for story time which features a disabled child and have dolls, wheelchair, crutches and leg braces available to act out the story. Leave the toys out afterwards so that the children can develop their own stories.

- Introduce Persona Dolls. These are dolls with individual identities which are created when the dolls are first introduced – each one has its own family, home environment, background, likes, dislikes and personality. The dolls can be used to introduce the subject of disability, but they can also be used to deal with situations which arise as they give children the opportunity to discuss issues and find positive solutions. Persona Doll stories can support children and help them to develop understanding, acceptance and positive attitudes towards diversity.

6 Taking part in assessment and statementing

For some children, any help offered by their setting through Early Years Action Plus (see page 43) will not be sufficiently effective to enable them to progress satisfactorily.

For these children, a multi-disciplinary assessment will be required in order to identify and help meet their needs. This means that a number of professionals, including an educational psychologist, will be called upon to produce evidence that describes that child's particular needs – all in consultation with the parents.

Parents, schools and settings can make a request to the local education authority (LEA) for a statutory assessment. However, settings in receipt of government funding to provide early education (other than maintained nursery schools or nursery classes in maintained schools) currently only have the statutory right to request an assessment for four and five year olds for whom they provide nursery education.

Once the assessment has identified a child's needs, the process by which they will be met is set out in a document called a 'statement'. Where needs are severe and complex, a request for assessment may be made prior to attendance at an early years setting so that some children may arrive at the setting with a statement already in place.

The assessment and statementing process sounds deceptively easy. But for many parents it is the start of what can seem like an uphill bureaucratic struggle to obtain what they think is best for their child. It is a system which often seems to require that parents describe the children they love through a number of impersonal definitions, none of which encompasses or adequately describes them. For some, it also means reliving the trauma of diagnosis.

Statutory assessment may not always result in a statement. The information gained during an assessment may indicate other ways in which the setting can meet the child's needs without the need for this.

Assessment process

According to the revised Code of Practice, an LEA should involve parents, educational settings and other appropriate agencies when considering whether a statutory assessment is necessary. If it is judged to be so, the assessment should then be conducted in close collaboration with them.

There are three routes to referral:

1 a request from the child's school or setting
2 a request from a parent
3 a referral by another agency, such as social services.

When making a request the child's setting should clearly state the reasons for the request and submit the following evidence:

- the views of parents recorded at Early Years Action and Early Years Action Plus or, if the action stages are not considered sufficient for the child, the reasons why the setting has decided to move directly to a request for assessment
- the ascertainable views of the child
- copies of relevant IEPs (see page 42)
- evidence of progress over time
- copies of advice, where provided, from health and social services

- evidence of the involvement and views of external professionals
- evidence (contained in IEPs and other relevant documentation) of the extent to which the school or setting has followed the advice of relevant external professionals.

While the LEA is considering whether to make a statutory assessment, parents should receive from the LEA:

- a full explanation of the process and the time limits that operate
- an invitation to submit written and/or oral evidence related to their child's assessment
- details of a named LEA officer from whom they can receive further information
- information about the LEA Parent Partnership Service which should be able to offer advice, information and support.

When a child is brought to the attention of the LEA by a request for a statutory assessment, the LEA must decide within six weeks whether to carry out such an assessment. Factors in addition to academic assessment that the LEA must also take account of are:

- any evidence that the child's performance is different in different environments
- evidence of contributory medical problems
- evidence from assessments or interventions by child health or social services.

Once a concern is agreed as valid, the LEA should collect reports from the setting(s) that the child is attending, to which relevant playgroup or nursery staff should be able to contribute. They will also elicit reports from an educational psychologist and relevant medical professionals (for example medical consultant, speech therapist, physiotherapist, occupational therapist, health visitor), as appropriate.

The statutory procedures for assessment are set out in detail in Chapter 7 of the Code of Practice (Department of Education and Skills 2001b). This process should usually take no longer than 26 weeks.

Children under compulsory school age and over two

For children who fall into this category, the LEA must consider the following questions when deciding whether a statutory assessment is required:

- What difficulties have been identified by the setting?
- What individualised strategies have been used during Early Years Action and Early Years Action Plus?
- Has outside advice been sought regarding the child's:
  - physical health and functioning
  - communication skills
  - perceptual and motor skills
  - self-help skills
  - social skills
  - emotional and behavioural development
  - responses to learning experiences?
- Have parental views been considered?

If the LEA decides that the statutory procedures are essential in order to maximise opportunity for an individual child, they will follow the same statementing process as for older children (see Department for Education and Skills 2001b, Chapter 7). Parents have a right at this stage to express a preference for the setting that is specified in the statement, so the LEA should ensure that parents have full information on the range of provision available and be given opportunities to visit. Parents should be able to discuss any aspect of provision with their named LEA officer.

LEAs should consider informal reviews of the statement for a child under five every six months, to ensure the provision is still appropriate.

Children under two

Statements are rarely issued for children under two years. The LEA is required to consider individual programmes of support according to a child's particular needs and these procedures are not specified in legislation. Very young children may need access to a home-based programme, such as Portage, or other peripatetic services, and in some cases Sure Start programmes may already have coordinated access to relevant services. As with all arrangements for children, this will very much depend on which services are available locally as these vary enormously from place to place.

If the LEA believes that a child has, or probably has, special educational needs, it may assess the child, given parental consent. If the parents request an assessment, the LEA must comply unless it believes that an assessment is not necessary (Education Act 1996, Section 175).

At this age assessment need not follow the statutory procedures that apply for older children; their guidance comes instead from the Code of Practice.

If a decision is made to issue a statement because of the complexity of a child's needs, or to allow them access to a particular service it should include:

- all available information about the child, with a clear specification of the child's special educational need
- a record of the views of parents and relevant professionals
- a clear account of the services being offered, including the contribution of the education service, the educational

objectives to be secured and the contribution of any statutory or voluntary agencies

- a description of the arrangements for monitoring and review.

Moving to primary school

Some children will require a statement prior to entering primary school. Any record drawn up by an early education setting should be passed to the school, with the parents' consent.

Parents' rights

It is very important for parents to make a full contribution to the assessment process. Parents must be consulted by the LEA and have the right to make a written declaration, which practitioners may be able to help with (see 'Parents' written contribution to assessment', page 87). Parents' intuitive feelings about their children should never be underestimated, but it is also important for them to try to explain why they feel as they do so that they can give as full a picture as possible of the child. In supporting parents as they write their contribution, it may also be helpful to ask them the following questions:

- How do you compare your child with others of the same age?
- What is your child good at? What does he or she enjoy?
- What does your child worry about? Is he or she aware of difficulties?
- What are your worries or concerns?
- Are there any major life changes or events that should be taken into consideration?

- What do you think your child's special educational needs might be and how would you like them to be provided for?

Parents are legally entitled to be given language support and any other kind of help they need in order to understand and participate in the process. They can also request that any independent professional reports they have obtained regarding their child should be included in the assessment.

Parents should be informed that they have a right to attend all their children's examinations, including psychological assessment, so long as it is felt to be in the child's best interest.

The view of the child

The Code of Practice says that children have a right to be heard. They should be encouraged to participate in decision-making about provision to meet their needs as part of a lifelong process of self-advocacy. Ascertaining young children's views may not be easy, but the principle should nevertheless be applied. Speech and language difficulties can often be overcome using specialist strategies. The publication, *Having a say: disabled children and effective partnership in decision making* (Russell and Beecher 1998) was a comprehensive review of different approaches to involving children, including young children, in decision-making. (See also 'Disabled children and choice', pages 10–11.)

Statementing

If, following assessment, the LEA decides that a child requires extra provision, it needs to consider what form it will take, whether it can be made within the given setting's existing resources or whether a statement is necessary.

Parents' written contribution to assessment

A written contribution can be as short or long as parents wish.
If you are helping a parent with this, it is much better to
approach it from what the child can do rather than focusing
exclusively on what the child can't do. The following headings
may be helpful, and are directed as if asked to the parents
(adapted from Wolfendale 1989a).

The earliest years
- What was the child like as a young baby?
- Were you happy about the child's progress at the time?
- When did you begin to feel worried?
- What happened to make you feel this?
- Did you receive any help or advice? If so, from whom?

What is the child like now?
General health
- eating and sleeping
- general fitness
- absences from school, playgroup, etc.
- any accidents or periods of illness
- any medicine or special diet

Physical skills
- crawling, walking, jumping, running
- climbing stairs
- catching
- building bricks
- doing jigsaws
- scribbling, drawing, writing

Self-help
- dressing, undressing
- feeding, eating
- toileting
- brushing teeth and hair
- washing hands and face
- wiping nose

Communication
- gestures, pointing
- sounds
- single words, phrases
- general comprehension
- descriptive powers

(Note: Children whose first language is not English often undergo a period of relative non-communication while they absorb vocabulary and syntax.)

Playing and learning at home
- favourite toys and activities
- concentration levels
- playing alone and with others
- stories

Relationships
- with parents
- with brothers and sisters
- with friends
- with other adults at home and outside
- is the child a loner?

Behaviour at home
- cooperation and sharing
- good and bad moods
- demonstrations of affection
- sulking or temper tantrums
- routine and rules

Behaviour at school, nursery, playgroup, childminder
- relationships with other children and adults
- progress with reading, writing and other subjects
- whether the child is settled and enjoying life
- what the child finds easy or hard

The proposed statement

If the LEA decides that a statement is required, they must first draw up a proposed statement. This should not contain any details of where the proposed educational provision will be made, as the LEA must first send the proposed statement and copies of any advice submitted during the assessment to the child's parents and all those who submitted advice.

At the same time, the LEA must send the parents a notice setting out the procedures to be followed, including arrangements for the choice of provision and the parents' rights, including that of appeal to the SEN tribunal (see 'SEN tribunal', page 90). LEAs need to make arrangements to support parents whose first language is not English and/or for different cultural backgrounds.

On receipt of the proposed statement, parents have a right to state a preference for provision and to raise any other issues relating to the body of the statement. Parents have 15 days in which to give the LEA their opinions, or to ask for a meeting with an LEA officer or any professional who gave advice during the assessment. They may ask for a delay of 14 to 21 days in order to gain further professional advice, or if they need more time to consider. Further meetings can be arranged, providing the request is made within 15 days of the last meeting.

The LEA must usually issue the final statement within eight weeks of the proposed statement.

Difficulties can arise around the level of specialised provision, or the terms of a recommendation can sometimes be so general that they are meaningless. For instance, 'provide access to speech therapy or physiotherapy' means very little in real terms as these services are often recommended according to available resources rather than the level of need. Such provision needs to be quantified in terms of number of hours per week or month. Parents who run into these difficulties should seek specialist advice from one of the agencies listed in Appendix 1.

What does the statement look like?

A statement should describe the nature of the child's special educational need, and all the help he will require as a consequence. A statement of SEN is set out in six parts:

- Part 1 sets out appropriate information about the family and lists the advice received during statutory assessment.
- Part 2 gives details about all of the child's SEN, as identified in the statutory assessment.
- Part 3 describes all the special help that the LEA thinks the child should receive in order to meet the needs listed in Part 2. It should also describe the long-term aims and arrangements for setting short-term goals, and describe how the child's progress is to be monitored.
- Part 4 describes the provision (for example early years setting or school) and any other arrangements that are being made.
- Part 5 describes any non-educational needs that the child has, as agreed between the LEA, local authority health department, social services and any other relevant agency.
- Part 6 sets out how the child's non-educational needs, as set out in Part 5, will be met.

The final statement

When the proposed statement has been agreed, the final statement is issued, and a copy sent to parents. This statement now includes details of where provision for the child will be made.

If the statement is agreed, the LEA should organise the provision set out as soon as possible. If the statement is not agreed, parents have the right of appeal to the SEN tribunal.

SEN tribunal

The special educational needs tribunal is an independent body set up to hear parental appeals on statutory assessments and statements. Tribunals should be held locally and the panel will consist of three people, including a lawyer and two others who have appropriate experience of special educational needs and local government.

Although these tribunals were set up under recent legislation to be less intimidating than previous systems, lay people involved – and parents in particular – sometimes find it an ordeal. Parents will usually need the support of a friend, independent parental supporter or named person who can help them prepare the case and accompany them to the hearing.

The tribunal will look at all the evidence and consider how the LEA's actions and recommendations compare with the guidance given in the Code of Practice. Their decision is binding on the LEA.

Revising a statement

Children, and young children in particular, can change very quickly and suddenly close developmental gaps. For children under five, the LEA should informally review the statement at least every six months, to ensure that the provision is still appropriate to the child's needs.

The LEA can review a statement at any time as long as the parents and school agree, and their agreement is sought every year (Section 172 (5) of the Code of Practice). This might be done through an annual meeting to assess the child's progress towards agreed targets and review the appropriateness of provision.

Parents should be given appropriate support and full information well before the meeting, including who is attending and why they are there.

How early years practitioners can help with assessment and statementing

1 Be observant. Make sure that you have an effective method of record-keeping in place.
2 Get to know the assessment and statementing process by reading the Code of Practice (Department of Education and Skills 2001b), and the parent's guide to the Code of Practice for your group.
3 Be a good communicator. Don't let your worries about a child build up. Talk to parents, and know when you need support yourself and where to find it.
4 Focus on the positives regarding the child, on what he or she can do instead of what he or she can't.
5 Find out who the key professionals are in your area and make contact, where appropriate (see Chapter 8).
6 Be a good listener. Recognise that many parents experience tremendous anxiety during the assessment and statementing process.
7 Find out as much as you can about local voluntary organisations and parent partnership schemes (see Appendix 1).
8 Appoint a key person in your group with responsibility for special needs (SENCO), but make sure that the rest of you are knowledgeable too.
9 Take advantage of any relevant training opportunities that come your way; even the most experienced member of staff will benefit.
10 Remember how much difference early support can make, both to the child and to the family.

Choosing suitable provision

When parents are choosing provision for a child, their decision will probably be based on a combination of things, including their own experiences as children, their practical needs as a family, and what they feel is right for their individual child. Such decisions are never easy, but parents of disabled children often find they have an additional hurdle to leap because there is usually less choice available to them. Access to information about services and parents' rights can help a great deal at this stage.

Pre-school children

Under the Children Act 1989, local authorities are required to produce information about local provision for parents, and to make it freely available. Details of services for disabled children should be included. Local authorities have children's information services, and comprehensive national and local information is available from ChildcareLink (see Appendix 1). Early Years Development and Childcare Partnerships are also required to hold appropriate lists of providers, and may be approached for information and advice.

Nurseries, day care, playgroups or other types of early years provision are now required to have a written policy on special educational needs. Local advisers can help parents sort through and understand these policies, and local parents with disabled children will have useful advice about how the policies of individual settings work in practice.

School-age children

As part of their statutory duties, governing bodies of all maintained schools must publish information about, and report on, the school's policy on special educational needs.

This should include:

- basic information about the school's special educational provision
- information about the school's policy for identification, assessment and provision for all pupils with special educational needs
- information about the school's staffing policies and partnership with bodies beyond the school.

The school's annual report from governors must include information on how effective the policy has been and how effective the school system is in all the relevant areas.

The National Curriculum

The National Curriculum, introduced in all schools by the Education Act 1988, includes children with special educational needs. The Act requires all schools, including special schools, to provide a balanced and broadly based curriculum which promotes the spiritual, moral, cultural, mental and physical development of pupils at the school and in society, and prepares pupils for the opportunities, responsibilities and experiences of adult life.

The curriculum guidance for the Foundation Stage (Department for Education and Employment and Qualifications and Curriculum Authority 2000) states that 'no child should be excluded or disadvantaged because of ethnicity, culture or religion, home language, family background, special educational needs, disability, gender or ability'.

Sharing information

The requirements in the Code of Practice for record-keeping are described on page 41, but it is also important to think about the day-to-day information you need.

How much information do you need?

It is unlikely that you will need to know a lot about a child's specific condition, but you *do* need practical information to help you care for him or her. This might include details about how he or she likes or needs to be handled, any dietary requirements, drugs to be administered and how much the child can see or hear.

Avoid the temptation to find out about each syndrome or condition, as this reinforces the medical model of disability. You need to know if a child has epilepsy, but it is more important to find out how this affects the child as an individual than to gather a lot of general information about the syndrome which has caused it.

Who needs to know?

It is unlikely that every member of staff needs to know everything about the child. When sharing information about a child, consider who really needs to know it in order to ensure the child's wellbeing in your setting.

Some children have behaviour which challenges us – serious biting, for example. This can cause some difficulty when deciding who to tell. On the one hand, if people are told of this behaviour before meeting the child, it will inevitably affect their attitude. But if you do not share the information and they are bitten, they may feel let down when they realise that you knew this was likely to happen.

A clear policy statement of the principles behind sharing information among staff members can help avoid this kind of difficulty.

7 Working with parents

Parents hold key information about their child's abilities, character, particular needs, life experiences, health, likes and dislikes, their place in the family and their cultural world. This information is vital if staff are to enable an individual child to progress. Building a strong and positive relationship from the start reduces the risk of misunderstanding and conflict later on.

The reasons for working closely with parents of disabled children are much the same as for working with all parents. However, it is important to understand that the experience of this group of parents, and the context in which they are parenting, may be different from that of a family with a non-disabled child.

Parents of disabled children are sometimes alienated by the amount and quality of professional intervention they have already received. They are often seen as over-protective and anxious for their children and we must take account of situations and experiences in the past which may have given rise to these worries and insecurities, even if we are sometimes justified in considering their reactions to be inappropriate.

Many parents of disabled children have experienced grief as part of the process of coming to terms with their child's disability. They grieved for their expectations, and experienced a sense of loss for the child they expected to have. Some parents may be beginning to grieve, or still in the process of grieving; for some parents, it may seem impossible to move on from shock, anger and denial. A sensitive and understanding approach is essential to enable parents to work through these feelings.

Many parents are struggling to overcome the effects of negative interpretations of disability, which are all too often reinforced by the attitudes and assumptions of those around them (see 'The medical model', page 6). At times, parents of disabled children are sad, angry, hostile and confused, and who could blame them?

Encountering professionals who have a positive attitude and who embrace the social model of disability can be an important step in the right direction (see 'The social model', page 6). It is also important to remember that any information regarding services or a child's condition is best given when the parent is in an emotional state which allows them to receive and absorb the information being given.

Why work with parents?

To understand the value of working with parents, it is important to look at the potential benefits for the children and the staff educating and caring for them.

It is crucial for every child's sense of wellbeing and self-esteem that her main carers – her parents – are accepted and valued by staff, and disabled children are no exception. Research has proved that a child's sense of identity and confidence is reinforced if staff and parents work as partners.

For practitioners, power-sharing, and the awareness and maturity to learn from parents, can enhance and develop working practice. It is valuable for staff to see how parents view a particular issue regarding the care and education of their child, rather than to adopt a prescriptive approach that does not take this into account.

It is also very important to share information with parents on progress and things that happen while the child is in your service. Home–centre diaries, which travel backwards and forwards with the child, are valuable provided they are not seen as a boring daily task. Avoid repetition; it is much better to have short entries than long ones which say the same as the day before, and the day before that. Staff should also record problems and setbacks as well as positive things, otherwise parents may feel inadequate because they think that staff are not experiencing any problems.

Remember that talking to parents is a very good way of sharing information.

Ideas for links between home and early years settings

- Outreach home visits.
- A toy and resource library from which children and parents can borrow.
- Early years curriculum workshops for professionals and parents.
- A bookshelf and/or notice-board with useful pamphlets on many topics, including SEN.
- An open-door policy for parents to call in and talk with staff at mutually convenient times.
- Story sessions by parents and extended family members.
- Opportunities for parents to share any specialist skills with the children.
- A refreshment and social room/corner for parents and younger family members.
- Appropriate parent education programmes and/or discussion groups.

(Adapted from Mortimer 2001)

What about partnership?

Those of us who work with parents of disabled children are constantly exhorted to be 'partners'. The concept is at best a slippery one. Sheila Wolfendale (1989b) describes the building blocks for partnership to be as follows:

- equality in decision-making
- power-sharing
- equal rights in self-expression
- the exercise of mutual responsibility and accountability by all parties.

While these are noble goals, they are rarely evident in the early experiences of parents with disabled children.

It is probable that we have not yet seen the empowerment of parents on a scale necessary to underpin real partnership, although there are many ways of doing so. We need to give parents access to local and global information. We need to promote disability equality training, and increase parents' assertiveness skills. We also need to set up parents' forums and have flexible meeting times backed up by childcare. Above all we must listen and be prepared to act on what we hear.

Becoming an ally

The concept of being an ally is just as important as that of partnership. It puts professionals in an auxiliary role, with parents and children at the head of the wider team.

The concept of being an ally means that power is not only shared, but weighted towards disabled adults, children and their families. The term has been adopted by the Disability Movement, to describe the input they require from the non-disabled population and it is a model which could usefully underpin the future development of disabled people's rights.

Micheline Mason, a disabled campaigner and the parent of a disabled child puts it like this:

> The truth is this: we do need you, not to be 'experts' or managers of our lives, but to be friends, enablers and receivers of our gifts to you. We need you to admit cheerfully what you don't know, without shame, to ask us what we need before providing it, to lend us your physical strength when appropriate, to allow us to teach you necessary skills; to champion our rights, to remove barriers previously set in place, to return to us any power you may have had over our lives.
>
> (Reiser and Mason 1992)

Working with disabled parents

> *A disabled parent is any parent who has a physical or sensory impairment, chronic illness or learning difficulty and whose experience of parenting is affected by the inappropriate design of buildings, external environments and facilities designed for family use or by discriminatory attitudes and/or actions.*
>
> Definition used by ParentAbility to the All Party Disablement Group 1996

The exact number of disabled parents in the UK is not known and this very absence of reliable statistics has caused the needs of this important minority to be neglected. They are an invisible group which is rarely acknowledged within society. Their job as parents is generally unsupported by mainstream services, especially childcare provision, or by the education system which may be accessible to their children but excludes them.

The lack of awareness in both the planning and delivery of services can further disadvantage parents already struggling within a hostile system. It is important to take the needs of disabled parents into account during the process of planning, policy-making and the dissemination of information within your group. Think about the needs of disabled parents when arranging meetings.

- Are the building and the meeting room accessible to wheelchair users?
- Are signs clearly visible, and does the parent need to sit at the front so they can see and hear what is happening?
- Is a sign language interpreter required?

Think, too, about how you provide information.

- Does the parent need documents to be provided in Braille, large print or audiotape versions?
- Would they find it helpful if you talked through the information with them?

It is important, too, that disabled children are given positive role models of disabled adults living full and responsible lives.

8 Guide to professionals involved with families

The range of professionals involved with an individual family will vary according to the level and type of need. However, it is likely that disabled children and their families will have had to cope with a much greater level of professional input than families of non-disabled children ever experience. This can be a help, a hindrance or sometimes even both, depending on the sensitivity and experience of the individual professional and on the appropriateness of the service itself.

While some professionals are part of a team, others work individually. What they share is the fact that they are involved with the child and the family. All those who share in the care and education of a particular child are part of this wider team.

Communication, as we all know, can be a tricky business. In the weeks following diagnosis, some families of disabled children have the unfortunate experience of being visited by 10 or even 20 different professionals. Each will have expressed sympathy, and offered help and advice, some of it conflicting. These early experiences are very important for families, as this is when a positive attitude and trust should be built up. At this stage a sensitive, efficient, supportive and resourceful professional can make a real impact on a family's future experience and expectations.

It is also important to remember that while services should empower parents, they should intrude as little as possible on family life. Families have the right to refuse services that do not meet their needs or become intrusive.

At the other end of the spectrum, there are still areas of the country where services are patchy or non-existent. However efficient the system in a particular area, there will be a significant number of families who fall through the net. These families have to battle through each day with very little support or information. It is vital to encourage them to ask for help, as they may well have become angry and alienated by their experiences. Practitioners involved with disabled children and their families should therefore be aware of:

- the identity of relevant professionals
- the nature of the service that they provide
- how this service should fit into the pattern of overall care
- the channels by which they might liaise with them if the situation required it.

Professionals who may have contact with families

This is a checklist of the professionals who might be involved with an individual family at any given time. Remember that the availability of services will vary a great deal from area to area.

- **Audiologist** – works with children and adults with hearing loss who are experiencing speech or language problems, to enable them to communicate.
- **Clinical psychologist** – works with children and their families to help with any developmental and behavioural problems.
- **Counsellor** – helps families come to terms with the emotional impact of disability.
- **Educational psychologist** – deals with all aspects of special educational need, sometimes in a clinical situation,

although they are often available to settings as a resource and may also have a training role.

- **Genetic counsellor** – helps families determine their risk factors for future children.
- **Health visitor** – provides a home-visiting, primary care service which may be specialist or generic, according to area policy.
- **Occupational therapist** – deals with all aspects of life skills and provides physical aids when appropriate.
- **Orthoptist** – works with children and adults who have squints, vision problems and abnormal eye movements.
- **Paediatrician** – doctor who specialises in working with children.
- **Parent partnership officer (PPO)** – usually employed by the LEA, the PPO liaises with parents on all aspects of SEN while the child is at school, and supports parents through the process of assessment, statementing, review and transition.
- **Physiotherapist** – deals with the physical aspects of a child's development.
- **Portage worker** – provides a home-visiting, educational service.
- **Social worker** – helps with the practical aspects such as applying for benefits, respite care and household adaptations.
- **Special educational needs coordinator (SENCO)** – the individual in a school or setting who has been designated as having responsibility for special educational needs.
- **Speech therapist** – supports all aspects of language development.

From this list of professionals, there are some who are particularly useful for families with disabled children, whose services are outlined below. It is a good idea for early years settings to forge contacts with these local professionals (see also Appendix 1 for contact details).

Health visitors

Some health authorities employ specialist health visitors to work with disabled children. If these specialists do not exist in your health authority, the generic health visitors will have special needs as part of their normal caseload. In both instances, health visitors are the individuals most likely to have in-depth knowledge of a child's family circumstances. A good health visitor will monitor the support given by other professionals to the family and help them regulate visits. They will also recognise the need for social integration and encourage contact with neighbours, local families in similar circumstances and other support networks. The health visitor can also be a crucial contact when it comes to referrals.

Portage services

Portage is an early intervention programme that uses home-visiting to support parents in the care and development of their child. Portage workers are trained to focus on what a child can do rather than what they can't do. They collaborate with parents to design appropriate activities to support development in the relevant areas, for example to stimulate very early motor skills or help with complex areas of development such as language.

As Portage is supplied to a family through a consistent worker or workers, a trusting relationship is often formed so that other issues are also discussed. Where Portage exists, it can be extremely successful in helping the family come to terms with grief and to develop a positive attitude through the experience of mutual respect and parent–professional partnership.

Child development teams

These are multi-disciplinary teams, usually based in one location. The term child development centre brings together all the different professionals who may then work cooperatively with a particular child. Some centres provide a one-stop service that will also deal with assessment. Making your group known to this team will help to provide the continuum of care that families desperately need.

Speech therapist, occupational therapist and physiotherapist

These professionals are all engaged in supporting the development of individual children. If you are caring for a child in any capacity, you are also part of that team. It is important to provide continuity for children in these areas and if you cannot find an opportunity to form a working relationship with them directly, make sure you find out what approach they recommend for any child in your care by asking the child's parents.

Parent partnership services

Every local authority should now have a parent partnership officer and/or service. The parent partnership officer can be an extremely useful resource for both providers and parents. Their job is to support and liaise with parents regarding all aspects of their child's education.

Understanding professionals

Over time or through training, most relevant professionals will have evolved a technique of responding to disability. While there are many excellent professionals who act as allies to disabled children and their families, you will almost certainly hear complaints from parents about their treatment by individual practitioners.

Because of the lack of disability equality training and institutional awareness, many professionals have not had a chance to explore the feelings that may underlie their practices and beliefs. Heavy caseloads may leave little space for self-exploration and reflective time.

We all carry historically accumulated emotional baggage as part of our response to disability; those who work in the field, for all or part of the time, are no exception. These deep-seated, unrecognised fears and prejudices may have a subconscious influence even if they have been discarded intellectually.

For this and other complex and personal reasons some professionals are more able than others to react constructively, and to find positive ways of helping a family. Appropriate training, counselling and disability awareness are needed to help all professionals explore their motivations and practice. On a positive note, most families will also have experience of a key professional who has provided a lifeline in helping the family pull through a difficult situation or crisis.
Under the social model of disability, we all carry the responsibility and the capacity to counter prejudice and misunderstanding.

Parents are experts

It is essential not to forget that parents should be a valued source of information. Not only are they the primary educators of their children, but they are also experts on their physical, social and emotional requirements.

Yes, parents are fallible, but this is a common feature of all experts. What is important is that you grow in knowledge together from a position of mutual respect.

Appendix 1
Help, information and advice

Many families report great difficulty in gaining access to information, whether relating to the nature of the child's condition or about services which may be available to improve the quality of life for the family.

Sometimes this information has already been made available to families, but in an unhelpful form, or at a time when parents are not able to absorb it, such as when they were first given a diagnosis of their child's condition.

Without adequate information, many parents feel disempowered and unable to make the right choices. Families often have difficulty in establishing an adequate level of practical and financial help. The benefits system, for example, is a maze and it can be difficult for parents to maintain paid employment because of the level of physical care they must provide for their children. Later on, families may face problems securing the kind of educational provision that they feel is appropriate for their child.

Helping families gain access to the right information is one of the single most important contributions that early years practitioners can make towards improving their quality of life. The list in this section includes organisations that will be able to help parents directly, and also which can inform and advise practitioners.

Children's Information Services

There is a Children's Information Service (CIS) in each local
authority area. CISs provide parents with information about
childcare available in the area, and they make it available in
local centres such as surgeries, supermarkets, libraries and
colleges as well as the CIS offices. Many CISs have
computerised databases and provide parents with guidance on
choosing and assessing childcare providers. Details of local
CISs and of all local childcare can be found through
ChildcareLink (see page 112).

Local directories

Under the 1989 Children Act, all local authorities must
produce information for parents regarding local services. In
many authorities this comes in the form of an Under-eights
Directory and this, or its local equivalent, should include
information about services for families with disabled children.

Useful addresses and information

Key:
☎ Telephone number
☎ Helpline
💻 Website
✉ Email

Action for Leisure
c/o Warwickshire College
Moreton Morrell Centre
Moreton Morrell
Warwickshire CV35 9BL
☎ 01926 650195
Resource centre, information
leaflets, advice and training.

Advisory Centre for Education
1b Aberdeen Studios
22 Highbury Grove
London N5 2DQ
☎ 020 7354 8321
☎ 0808 800 5793
💻 www.ace-ed.org.uk
Offers guidance on all aspects
of education. They will forward
a publications list on request.

AFASIC (Association for all Speech Impaired Children)
50–52 Great Sutton Street
London EC1V 0DJ
☎ 020 7490 9410
☎ 0845 3 55 55 77
💻 www.afasic.org.uk
Charity representing children
and young adults with
communication impairments,
working for their inclusion in
society and supporting their
parents and carers.

All Together Training and Consultancy
70b Lady Somerset Road
London NW5 1TU
☎ 020 7482 1165
✉ marydickins@btinternet.com
Independent Training and
Consultancy on all aspects of
the provision of inclusive
services for young children and
their families.

Key:
☎ Telephone number
☎ Helpline
🖳 Website
✉ Email

Alliance for Inclusive Education
Unit 2
70 South Lambeth Road
London SW8 1RL
☎ 020 7735 5277
🖳 www.allfie.org.uk
National network of individuals, families and groups who campaign for inclusive education.

ASBAH (Association for Spina Bifida and Hydrocephalus)
42 Park Road
Peterborough PE1 2UQ
☎ 01733 555988
🖳 www.asbah.org
ASBAH aims to improve services for people with spina bifida and/or hydrocephalus, to work with them to extend their choices, and maximise opportunities for independence and achievement. A network of professional advisers provides advice and practical support to people with these disabilities, their families and carers.

Association of Parents of Vaccine Damaged Children
78 Campden Road
Shipston-on-Stour
Warwickshire CV36 4DH
☎ 01608 661595
An association of parents mainly concerned with obtaining adequate compensation for children damaged by vaccination. It also offers support to families.

Carers UK
20–25 Glasshouse Yard
London EC1A 4JT
☎ 020 7490 8818
☎ 0808 808 7777
🖳 www.carersonline.org.uk
Information and advice for carers.

Centre for Accessible Environments
Nutmeg House
60 Gainsford Street
London SE1 2NY
☎ 020 7357 8182
🖳 www.cae.org.uk
An organisation which provides information to education providers and others on how the built environment can best be made, or modified, to achieve inclusion by design.

**Children's Play Information
Service**
National Children's Bureau
8 Wakley Street
London EC1V 7QE
☎ 020 7843 6303
A specialist resource providing
information on many aspects of
children's play, focusing on the
ages 5–14 years.

ChildcareLink
☎ 08000 96 02 96
🖳 www.childcarelink.gov.uk
National directory of local
childcare providers.

**CLAPA (Cleft Lip and Palate
Association)**
235–237 Finchley Road
London NW3 6LS
☎ 020 7431 0033
🖳 www.clapa.com
A partnership between parents
and health professionals
providing support for new
parents, and for people with
this condition and their families,
from infancy through to
adulthood. It is the only UK-
wide voluntary organisation
specifically helping those with
and affected by cleft lip and
palate.

**CLIMB (Children Living with
Inherited Metabolic Diseases)**
Climb Building
176 Nantwich Road
Crewe CW2 6BG
☎ 0870 7700 325
☎ 0870 7700 326
🖳 www.climb.org.uk
A national organisation working
on behalf of children, young
people, families, carers and
support groups affected by
metabolic diseases (genetic
disorders).

Contact a Family
209–211 City Road
London EC1V 1JN
☎ 020 7608 8700
☎ 0808 808 3555
🖳 www.cafamily.org.uk
General support for families
who care for disabled children,
including contact with other
families, information factsheets
and a newsletter.

Key:
☎ Telephone number
☎ Helpline
🖥 Website
✉ Email

Council for Disabled Children
National Children's Bureau
8 Wakley Street
London EC1V 7QE
☎ 020 7843 1900
Information, training, coordination and publications, including factsheets on services and facilities for disabled children, on leisure, respite care, education and holidays. Supports a network of Parent Partnership Officers.

CSIE (Centre for Studies on Integration in Education)
Room 2S203
S Block
Frenchay Campus
Coldharbour Lane
Bristol BS16 1QU
☎ 0117 344 4007
🖥 inclusion.uwe.ac.uk/csie/csiehome.htm
Information and advice about educating children with special needs in ordinary schools. They issue a series of factsheets, some free and some for a small charge.

Cystic Fibrosis Trust
11 London Road
Bromley
Kent BR1 1BY
☎ 020 8464 7211
🖥 www.cftrust.org.uk
Funds medical and scientific research aimed at understanding, treating and curing Cystic Fibrosis (CF). It also aims to ensure that people with CF receive the best possible care and support in all aspects of their lives.

Disability Equality in Education
Unit 4Q, Leroy House
436 Essex Road
London N1 3QP
☎ 020 7359 2855
🖥 www.diseed.org.uk
Training and resources for schools, colleges and local education authorities on the issue of inclusion for all students within the education system.

Disabled Parents Network
PO Box 5876
Towcester NN12 7ZN
☎ 0870 241 0450
🖥 www.disabledparentsnetwork.org.uk
A network of disabled parents which provides support to disabled people in pregnancy, childbirth and parenthood.

Down's Syndrome Association
155 Mitcham Road
London SW17 9PG
☎ 020 8682 4001
🖥 www.dsa-uk.com
Supports people with Down's
syndrome, their family and
carers as well as providing
information for those with a
professional interest. Also aims
to improve general
understanding and awareness of
the condition
and to champion the rights of
people with Down's syndrome.

High/Scope Institute UK
Copperfield House
190–192 Maple Road
London SE20 8HT
☎ 020 8676 0220
🖥 www.high-scope.org.uk
Information on the High/Scope
curriculum approach.

In Touch Trust
10 Norman Road
Sale
Cheshire M33 3DF
☎ 0161 905 2440
🖥 www.inclusive.co.uk/
support/intouch.shtml
Information and contacts for
parents of children with special
needs.

**IPSEA (Independent Panel for
Special Education Advice)**
6 Carlow Mews
Woodbridge
Suffolk IP12 1EA
☎ 01394 380518
☎ 0800 0184016
Independent expert advice for
parents who are uncertain
about, or disagree with, the
local education authority's
interpretation of their child's
special educational needs.

Kids
80 Waynflete Square
London W10 6UD
☎ 020 8969 2817
Provides a range of services
for families of disabled children
including family centres,
playgroups, holiday play
schemes.

Kidsactive
Pryor's Bank
Bishop's Park
London SW6 3LA
☎ 020 7736 4443
🖥 www.kidsactive.org.uk
Advice on play for disabled
children, magazine and
publications.

Key:
☎ Telephone number
☎ Helpline
🖳 Website
✉ Email

Kith & Kids
The Irish Centre
Pretoria Road
London N17 8DX
☎ 020 8801 7432
🖳 www.kithandkids.org.uk
Self-help group, with activities across London.

Mencap
123 Golden Lane
London WC1Y 0RT
☎ 020 7454 0454
🖳 www.mencap.org.uk
Voluntary organisation working with children and adults with a learning disability and their families and carers, to improve their lives and opportunities.

National Association of Toy and Leisure Libraries (Playmatters)
68 Churchway
London NW1 1LT
☎ 020 7387 9592
🖳 www.natll.org.uk
Supports existing toy and leisure libraries, promotes the development of new toy and leisure libraries and raises awareness of the importance of play.

National Autistic Society
393 City Road
London EC1V 1NG
☎ 020 7833 2299
🖳 www.nas.org.uk
Works to help people with autism live their lives with as much independence as possible.

National Deaf Children's Society
15 Dufferin Street
London EC1Y 8UR
☎ 020 7490 8656
☎ 0808 800 8880
🖳 www.ndcs.org.uk
Supports deaf children, young deaf people and their families in overcoming the challenges of childhood deafness.

National Development Team
Albion Wharf
Albion Street
Manchester M1 5LN
☎ 0161 228 7055
🖳 www.ndt.org.uk
Advises on services for children
and young people, and
provides consultancy to
voluntary organisations, health
authorities and NHS Trusts,
social services and education
departments.

National Portage Association
127 Monks Dale
Yeovil BA21 3JE
🖳 www.portage.org.uk
Portage is a home-visiting
educational service for parents
of young disabled children.

National Society for Epilepsy
Chesham Lane
Chalfont St Peter SL9 0RJ
☎ 01494 601300
☎ 01494 601400
🖳 www.epilepsynse.org.uk
Seeks to enhance the health
and wellbeing of people with
epilepsy by improving clinical
treatment and care and by the
provision of health information
to people with epilepsy, to
health professionals and the
general public.

Network 81
1–7 Woodfield Terrace
Stansted
Essex CM24 8AJ
☎ 0870 770 3262
☎ 0870 770 3306
🖳 www.network81.co.uk
A national network of parents
working towards properly
resourced inclusive education.

ParentAbility
Now part of the Disabled
Parents Network

**Parenting Education and
Support Forum**
Unit 431, Highgate Studios
London NW5 1TL
☎ 020 7824 8370
🖳 www.parenting-
forum.org.uk
Promotes and develops
parenting education and
support.

Parents at Work
45 Beech Street
London EC2Y 8AD
☎ 020 7628 3565
🖳 www.parentsatwork.org.uk
Offers practical information on
childcare options and ways of
balancing work and home. Has
researched the needs of parents
of children with disabilities who
are returning to work.

Key:
☎ Telephone number
☎ Helpline
🖥 Website
✉ Email

Parents for Inclusion
Unit 2
70 South Lambeth Road
London SW8 1RL
☎ 020 7735 7735
☎ 020 7582 5008
🖥 www.parentsforinclusion.org
Network of parents working for educational opportunities for children with special needs.

Parents With Attitude
PO Box 1727
Sheffield S11 7WS
🖥 www.parentswithattitude.
fsnet.co.uk

Playboard
59–65 York Street
Belfast BT15 1AA
☎ Telephone: 028 9080 3380
🖥 www.playboard.co.uk
Lead agency for all aspects of children's play in Northern Ireland.

Playlink
The Co-op Centre
Unit 5 Upper
11 Mowll Street
London SW9 6BG
☎ 020 7820 3800
Services include health and safety audits of playgrounds, training, consultancies, support and advice, resources and publications.

Pre-school Learning Alliance
69 Kings Cross Road
London WC1X 9LL
☎ 020 7833 0991
🖥 www.pre-school.org.uk
Main national organisation for playgroups and pre-schools.

REACT (Rapid Effectiveness Assistance for Children with Potentially Terminal Illness)
St Luke's House
270 Sandycombe Road
Kew
Richmond TW9 3NP
☎ 020 8940 2575
🖥 www.reactcharity.org
Helps children with life-limiting illness under the age of 18 living at home with their families.

Royal National Institute for Deaf People
19–23 Featherstone Street
London EC1Y 8SL
☎ 020 7296 8000
☎ 0808 808 0123
🖳 www.rnid.org.uk
Charity representing all deaf and hard of hearing people in the UK.

Royal National Institute for the Blind
105 Judd Street
London WC1H 9NE
☎ 020 7388 1266
☎ 0845 766 9999
🖳 www.rnib.org.uk
Practical support and advice to anyone with a sight problem.

SCOPE
6 Market Road
London N7 9PW
☎ 020 7619 7100
☎ 0808 800 3333
🖳 www.scope.org.uk
Society for people who have cerebral palsy.

Sense
11–13 Clifton Terrace
London N4 3SR
☎ 020 7272 7774
🖳 www.sense.org.uk
Organisation for people who are deafblind or have associated disabilities.

Sickle Cell Society
54 Station Road
London NW10 4UA
☎ 020 8961 7795
🖳 www.sicklecellsociety.org
Information, counselling and advice for those with sickle cell disorders and their families.

TAMBA (Twins and Multiple Births Association)
The Willows
Gardner Road
Guildford GU1 4PG
☎ 0870 770 3305
🖳 www.tamba.org.uk
Support for families with twins. Includes a Special Needs Families group.

Key:
☎ Telephone number
☎ Helpline
🖥 Website
✉ Email

Wellbeing

27 Sussex Place
Regent's Park
London NW1 4SP
☎ 020 7772 6400
🖥 www.wellbeing.org.uk
Supports research for healthier women and healthier babies.

WHIZZ-KIDZ, The Movement for Non-Mobile Children

1 Warwick Row
London SW1E 5ER
☎ 020 7233 6600
🖥 www.whizz-kidz.org.uk
Aims to help all types of disabled children to have improved mobility, increased independence and a greater quality of life. This is achieved by providing them with lightweight, powered and sports wheelchairs or any other mobility aid they may require.

Appendix 2
Training

There is still no formal qualification in this country specifically for early years practitioners who wish to work with disabled children. It is possible to choose options relating to SEN and disability issues at NVQ levels 3 and 4, but it is not mandatory.

Early years practitioners who are studying for degrees in early childhood studies or pursuing additional qualifications such as the Cache Advanced Diploma in Child Care and Education will have the opportunity to study the subject area in more depth.

Teachers, social workers and other related professionals involved with children may or may not have worked through a module on disability as part of their training. All too often the most they will get is a day or two of in-service training, although this situation is gradually improving.

According to the EYDCP planning guidance 2001–2002 (Department for Education and Skills 2001a), early years SENCOs should have benefited from an average of three days' relevant training by 2004. Most EYDCPs are now offering relevant continuing professional development workshops for early years practitioners and SENCOs as part of their training programmes. It is advisable to contact them directly, to see what is being made available locally.

Training in disability equality, inclusion and inclusive practice provides an opportunity to explore theory and attitudes, and how they relate to best practice. It would be preferable if this kind of training were a condition of employment in early years services, but for the moment, availability depends on local priorities.

If you are part of a large statutory or voluntary agency, you are better placed to press for your training needs to be met than if your group is small and isolated. In a small group, you will need to be inventive and resourceful in order to be equipped with the relevant skills and understanding.

Organisations that offer training are listed below, but the list is by no means exhaustive and cannot include local training initiatives.

Early years training

The following organisations run a range of courses, some of which are relevant to people working with young disabled children.

Key:
☎ Telephone number
☎ Helpline
🖥 Website
✉ Email

CACHE (Council for Awards in Children's Care and Education)
8 Chequer Street
St Albans AL1 3XZ
☎ 01727 847636
🖥 www.cache.org.uk

Children in Scotland
Princes House
5 Shandwick Place
Edinburgh EH2 4RG
☎ 0131 228 8484
🖥 www.childreninscotland.org.uk

National Children's Bureau
8 Wakley Street
London EC1V 7QE
☎ 020 7843 6000
🖥 www.ncb.org.uk

Play training

Some organisations offer training on play for disabled children and inclusion.

Action for Leisure
c/o Warwickshire College
Moreton Morrell Centre
Moreton Morrell
Warwickshire CV35 9BL
☎ 01926 650195

All Together Consultancy
✉ marydickens@btinternet.com

Kidsactive
Pryor's Bank
Bishop's Park
London SW6 3LA
☎ 020 7736 4443
🖥 www.kidsactive.org.uk

PLAY-TRAIN
31 Farm Road
Sparkbrook
Birmingham B11 1LS
☎ 0121 766 8446
🖥 www.playtrain.org.uk

Pre-school Learning Alliance
69 Kings Cross Road
London WC1X 9LL
☎ 020 7833 0991
🖥 www.pre-school.org.uk

Disability equality and awareness training

Disability equality training explores disability within the context of the social model (see page 6). The training is delivered by disabled trainers alone, or by disabled and non-disabled people working together. Contact the following organisations for further information.

Disability Equality in Education
Unit 4Q, Leroy House
436 Essex Road
London N1 3QP
☎ 020 7359 2855
🖥 www.diseed.org.uk

People First
299 Kentish Town Road
London NW5 2TJ
☎ 020 7485 6660
🖥 www.peoplefirstltd.com

Key:
☎ Telephone number
☎ Helpline
🖥 Website
✉ Email

Disability equality training (cont.)

Phab England
Summit House
Wandle Road
Croydon CR0 1DF
☎ 020 8667 9443
🖥 www.phabengland.org.uk

Training regarding specific disabilities

The following organisations often organise conferences and training events.

Asthma

National Asthma Campaign
Providence House
Providence Place
London N1 0NT
☎ 020 7226 2260
🖥 www.asthma.org.uk

Autism

National Autistic Society External Training and Consultancy
4th Floor, Castle Heights
72 Maid Marion Way
Nottingham NG1 6BJ
☎ 0115 911 3363
🖥 www.nas.org.uk

Down's syndrome

Down Syndrome Educational Trust [sic]
Sarah Duffen Centre
Belmont Street
Southsea PO5 1NA
☎ 023 9282 4261
🖥 www.downsed.org

Down's Syndrome Association
155 Mitcham Road
London SW17 9PG
☎ 020 8682 4001
🖥 www.dsa-uk.com

Dyslexia
British Dyslexia Association
98 London Road
Reading RG1 5AU
☎ 0118 966 2677
🖳 www.bda-dyslexia.org.uk

Eczema
National Eczema Society
Hill House
Highgate Hill
London N19 5NA
☎ 020 7281 3553
☎ 0870 241 3604
🖳 www.eczema.org

Emotional and behavioural difficulties
Association of Workers for Children with Emotional and Behavioural Difficulties
Charlton Court
East Sutton
Maidstone ME17 3DQ
☎ 01622 843104
🖳 www.awcebd.co.uk

Epilepsy
National Society for Epilepsy
Chesham Lane
Chalfont St Peter SL9 0RJ
☎ 01494 601300
☎ 01494 601400
🖳 www.epilepsynse.org.uk

Epilepsy Action
New Anstey House
Gate Way Drive
Yeadon
Leeds LS19 7XY
☎ 0113 210 8800
🖳 www.epilepsy.org.uk

Hearing impairment
National Deaf Children's Society
15 Dufferin Street
London EC1Y 8UR
☎ 020 7490 8656
☎ 0808 800 8880
🖳 www.ndcs.org.uk

Learning disabilities
British Institute of Learning Disabilities
Campion House
Green Street
Kidderminster
Worcestershire DY10 1JL
☎ 01562 723010
🖳 www.bild.org.uk

Key:
☎ Telephone number
☎ Helpline
🖳 Website
✉ Email

Visual impairment

Royal National Institute for the Blind

Education and Employment Centres

☎ London and South East:
020 7391 2304
☎ West Midlands:
0121 665 4200
☎ East Midlands:
0115 958 2322
☎ South West:
0117 953 7750
☎ North West:
0151 255 0562
☎ Yorkshire and Humberside:
0113 274 8855
☎ Scotland:
0131 311 8500
☎ Wales:
029 2045 0440
☎ Northern Ireland:
028 9032 9373
🖳 www.rnib.org.uk

Visits, placements and voluntary experience

One of the best ways of getting to know more about caring for disabled children is to get out into the world and find out for yourself. There may be various local services where you could spend some time as an observer or, even better, as a volunteer:

- opportunity group (playgroup which includes or caters for disabled children) or integrated pre-school
- group for parents and young children at a child development centre
- toy library
- special school
- specialist or integrated holiday playscheme.

You can find out about provision in your area from your local authority.

In London, the adventure playgrounds for disabled children run by Kidsactive offer placements that enable people to gain experience of working with disabled children. Contact Kidsactive for more details (see page 116).

Appendix 3
Suppliers of play and education equipment

Key:
- ☎ Telephone number
- ☎ Helpline
- 💻 Website
- ✉ Email

Education suppliers

Acorn Educational
32 Queen Eleanor Road
Geddington
Kettering NN14 1AY
☎ 01536 400212
💻 www.acorneducational.
co.uk

Formative Fun
Education House
Horn Park Business Centre
Broadwindsor Road
Beaminster DT8 3PT
☎ 01308 868999
💻 www.formative-fun.com

Galt Educational
Johnsonbrook Road
Hyde SK14 4QT
☎ 08451 20 30 05
💻 www.galt-educational.
co.uk

Hope Education
Hyde Buildings
Ashton Road
Hyde SK14 4SH
☎ 0845 120 2224
💻 www.hope-education.
co.uk

NES Arnold
Findel House
Excelsior Road
Ashby Park
Ashby de la Zouch LE65 1NG
☎ 0845 120 4525
💻 www.nesarnold.co.uk

Key:
☎ Telephone number
☎ Helpline
☏ Videophone
💻 Website
✉ Email

Rede Educational

153 Redehall Road
Burstow
Horley RH6 9RJ
☎ 01342 717538
💻 www.redeplay.co.uk

Step by Step

Lee Fold
Hyde SK14 4LL
☎ 0845 121 2205
💻 www.sbs-educational.co.uk

Special needs suppliers

Edu-play

29 Wigston Street
Counterthorpe
Leicester LE8 5RP
☎ 0116 277 2262

Rompa

Goyt Side Road
Chesterfield S41 0SW
☎ 01246 211777
💻 www.rompa.com

TFH

5–7 Severnside Business Park
Stourport-on-Severn
Worcestershire DY13 9HT
☎ 01299 827820
💻 www.tfhuk.com

Tocki

Hull Road
Eastrington
Goole DN14 7XL
Telephone: 01430 410515
💻 www.tocki.co.uk

Children's books suppliers

Blissymbol Communication UK

c/o Gillian Hazel
ACE Centre Advisory Trust
92 Windmill Road
Headington
Oxford OX3 7DR
☎ 01865 759800
✉ info@ace-centre.org.uk

ClearVision Project

Linden Lodge School
61 Princes Way
London SW19 6JB
☎ 020 8789 9575
💻 www.rnib.org.uk/clrvis

Community Insight
The Pembroke Centre
Cheney Manor
Swindon SN2 2PQ
☎ 01793 512612
🖳 www.c-insight.demon.
co.uk

Forest Bookshop Warehouse
Unit 2, New Building
Ellwood Road
Milkwall
Coleford GL16 7LE
☎ 01594 833858
☎ 01594 810637
🖳 www.forestbooks.com

Letterbox Library
71–73 Allen Road
London N16 8RY
☎ 020 7503 4801
🖳 www.letterboxlibrary.com

References and further reading

References

Booth, T and Ainscom M (2002) *Index for inclusion: developing learning and participation in schools.* CSIE

Cameron, J and Sturge Moore, L (1990) *Ordinary everyday families: a human rights issue.* Mencap Under-fives Project

Department for Education and Employment and Qualifications and Curriculum Authority (2000) *Curriculum guidance for the Foundation Stage.* DfEE and QCA

Department for Education and Skills (2001a) *Early Years Development and Childcare Partnership planning guidance 2001–2002.* DfES

Department for Education and Skills (2001b) *Special Educational Needs Code of Practice.* DfES

Department for Education and Skills (2001c) *SEN toolkit.* DfES

Greey, M (1994) *Honouring diversity: a cross-cultural approach to infant development for babies with special needs.* Centennial Infant and Child Centre

Lane, J (1999) *Action for racial equality in the early years.* National Early Years Network

Lear, R (1996) *Play helps: toys and activities for children with special needs.* 4th edn, Heinemann

Mason, M (1993) *Inclusion, the way forward: a guide to integration for young disabled children.* National Early Years Network

Mehrabian, A (1971) *Silent messages.* Wadsworth

Mortimer, H (2001) *Special needs and early years provision.* Continuum

Murray, P and Penman, J (1996) *Let our children be: a collection of stories.* Parents With Attitude

Ouvry, M (2003) *Exercising muscles and minds: outdoor play and the early years curriculum.* National Children's Bureau

Parents for Inclusion (2000) 'The Human Rights Act', *Parents for Inclusion newsletter.* Autumn, p. 6

Pettit, B and Laws, S (1997) *It's difficult to do dolls: images of disability in children's playthings.* Save the Children

Reiser, R and Mason, M (1992) *Disability equality in the classroom: a human rights issue.* Disability Equality in Education

Russell, P (1996) 'Putting disability discrimination issues firmly on the agenda', *Lets Play.* November

Russell, P and Beecher, W (1998) *Having a say: disabled children and effective partnership in decision making.* Council for Disabled Children

Save the Children (1992) *Equal opportunities: a guide to ensuring good practice on disability in UK fieldwork.* SCF

Stoneham, J (1996) *Grounds for sharing.* Southgate Publishers

Teacher Training Agency (1999) *National special educational needs specialist standards.* TTA

Thoreau, H D (1840) *Walden.* Currently available Oxford University Press, 1999

Wilson, R (1998) *Special educational needs in the early years.* Routledge

Wolfendale, S (1989a) *My child ... my story: guidelines to writing a parental profile.* Dorset County Council

Wolfendale, S (1989b) 'Parental involvement and power-sharing in special needs'. In S Wolfendale (ed.) *Parental involvement: developing networks between school, home and community.* Cassell

General reading

Department for Education and Skills (2001) *Special educational needs (SEN): a guide for parents and carers.* DfES

Jordan, L and Goodey, C (1996) *Human rights and school change: The Newham story.* Centre for Studies on Inclusive Education

Lang, G and Berberich, C (1995) *All children are special.* Eleanor Curtain Publishing

Miller, J (1997) *Never too young: how young children can take responsibility and make decisions.* National Early Years Network

Play and learning

Action for Leisure (2001) *Creative play: ideas to adapt creative play activities for disabled children and young people.* Action for Leisure

Action for Leisure (2001) *Storytime: ideas to make storytime an inclusive and sensory experience for disabled children and young people.* Action for Leisure

Beyer, J and Gammeltoft, L (2000) *Autism and play.* Jessica Kingsley

Coleman, M (2001) *Play it right!* RNIB

Kidsactive (2000) *Side by side: guidelines for inclusive play.* Kidsactive

Kidsactive (2002) *It doesn't just happen: inclusive management for inclusive play.* Kidsactive

Lear, R (1998) *Look at it this way: toys and activities for children with visual impairment.* Heinemann

Lear, R (1999) *Fingers and thumbs: toys and activities for children with hand-function problems.* Heinemann

Longhorn, F (1995) *A sensory curriculum for very special people.* Souvenir Press

Newman, S (1999) *Small steps forward: using games and activities to help your pre-school child with special needs.* Jessica Kingsley